*Charles Duncheon* (signature)

# REFLECTIONS OF A 5TH-GRADE GIRLS BASKETBALL COACH

## LIFE LESSONS FROM GIRLS' HOOPS

### CHARLIE DUNCHEON

PUBLISHED BY FASTPENCIL, INC.

Published by FastPencil, Inc.
3131 Bascom Ave.
Suite 150
Campbell CA 95008 USA
(408) 540-7571
(408) 540-7572 (Fax)
info@fastpencil.com
http://www.fastpencil.com

Characters appearing in Chapter 1 beyond the Los Gatos scene are fictitious. Any resemblance to real persons is purely coincidental.

The names of girls in some of the anecdotes have been changed to protect the innocent, and I do mean innocent.

To see reviews of this book visit:
www.charlieduncheon.posterous.com

To purchase signed copies of this book visit:
http://web.me.com/charlieduncheon

Second Edition

*To Casey, Sydney, and Dagney. Thanks for the memories.*

❧

# Acknowledgements

Thank you to all the girls I had the pleasure of coaching from 1996 to 2010 in Los Gatos, California, including teams from the Recreational League, the Calvary Church League, St. Mary's Grade School, National Junior Basketball (NJB) and NJB All Net. I can only hope that their experiences were as warm and rewarding as mine were. I thank my loving wife Dana who first talked me into coaching, which led to great basketball experiences with my three daughters and their wonderful teammates. I also thank my fellow volunteer coaches Steve Annen, Paul Beaupre, Jerry Bellotti, Derek Bowers, Michel Chmielewski, Dave Freitas, the late Bill Garfield, Pat Lacey, Jim and Kate McCaffrey, George Montanari, Truman Roe, Paul Simone, Joanne Varni, Mary Sue Penza, and Steve Smith who gave their valuable hours to the benefit of girls' basketball experience in Los Gatos. Lastly, I thank Fast Pencil and fellow Hoosier Melody Culver for teaching me how to publish a book.

# Contents

# PREFACE

I love basketball. I love my three daughters. That combination led me to one of the most enriching life experiences a guy could ever ask for. One night in 1998, my wife, Dana, asked why I was smiling when I got home from our oldest daughter Casey's fifth-grade basketball practice. She noticed that it was becoming a familiar pattern after practices. I told her about the funny things Casey and her teammate Janelle had done at practice. After a few more occasions of sharing laughs from practices and games, Dana encouraged me to write them down.

I hope you enjoy this short coaching (and personal) journey. I will share some of the joys and the heartaches, present tips on how to coach young girls' (and boys') basketball, offer some life lessons learned by the girls and by me, and pass on many of the amazing things that come out of the mouths of these wonderful young girls competing in the global game of basketball.

# 1

## WHAT A BEAUTIFUL GAME

"I have missed more than 9000 shots in my career. I have lost almost 300 games. On 26 occasions I have been entrusted to take the game winning shot ... and missed. And I have failed over and over and over again in my life. And that is why ... I succeed."

–Michael Jordan

In Shenzhen, China, on a late Friday February morning, young Chinese boys aged eleven to thirteen compete in a rigid training session on one of the thousands of new courts recently installed by the Chinese government. Lay-up drills and passing drills are conducted like a military exercise as the sun appears then disappears in a partly cloudy sky. The rigidity of the drills loosens up later, as the red shirt team plays a game against the white shirts. There are no smiles on the young faces, but they are smiling inside. All of them want to become famous basketball players like their hero, Yao Ming. The shortest player on the court dribbles past the tallest and makes a reverse lay-up. He breaks into the first smile of the day, showing a missing front tooth that may have been lost to an opponent's elbow. Five years ago he would have been a second priority compared to the taller player he just beat, but the Chinese have now learned that fast guards are just as important to develop as the tall "Mings." A lone government official taking notes at center court observes that this game has both promising forwards and fast, shorter guards.

Later that Friday in Melbourne, Australia, locals walk past the entrance of a gym and hear the constant squeaking of shoes on wood. The sources of the squeaks are ten girls ranging from ages sixteen to twenty-three, playing on a polished wood panel floor. All ten girls play intensely, with hopes of someday proudly representing their country in the Olympics and wearing the bright yellow jerseys with blue stars that form the Southern Cross. More than half the girls have blond hair bound in ponytails that match those jerseys. A tall, lean six-footer with curly red hair boxes out an even taller blonde, grasps the rebound from the missed shot and quickly whips the ball to the waiting Aussie girl in the wing. Another of a series of fast breaks ensues toward the other basket, as ten girls run full speed in the other direction, ten ponytails bobbing up and down in unison. Even the tenth girl, furthest from the girl making the lay-up, runs full speed toward the basket until she sees the ball fall through the net, then turns around to sprint full speed toward the other basket.

As that same sun now shines on Wau, Sudan, it relentlessly fries an outdoor asphalt court without a single square centimeter of shade. Eight young Sudanese boys with their black skin glistening in perspiration are going at it on one end of the court, oblivious to the heat or pebbles of sand blowing across the faded three-point line. Three more young boys wait under the only tree close to the court, a scraggly set of branches barely providing any shade for the boys or for the bottles of water taped with their names. Shoes (and in one case, sandals) slip on the sand, but every athlete gives 100% and never blames lost footing. One very thin fourteen-year-old defender anticipates a pass at the top of the key and intercepts the ball, moving full speed toward the other basket. He increases his lead on the other team as he passes the center line. Thoughts of Luol Deng, famous Sudanese basketball hero, float through his mind as he passes the three-point line,

then the free throw line. Picking up the dribble and putting both hands on the ball, he begins the launch off his
left foot for what he hopes is his first dunk. He slips on the
pebbled surface and goes crashing into the sandy terrain
just off the court. The ball rolls harmlessly in the sand
while laughter erupts from the other seven on the court
and three on the sidelines. Embarrassed, but showing his
bright white teeth in a broad grin, he gets up with sand
clinging to his bare back, shouting "next time!" in Arabic.

Later that day in Tuzla, Bosnia, a group of young girls
plays in an aged stone building with a faded tile floor. One
dark-haired girl by the name of Mila, wearing Mujanovic
on the back of her shirt, scores a putback and dreams of
playing for her country like her heroine, Razija Mujanovic.
Flakes of snow from the gray skies outside curl through a
broken window, but the heat of battle on the floor shows
no effect from the temperature. Despite aggressive man-
to-man defense, it seems that fast passing always finds an
Eastern European sharpshooter open to make a long
three-point shot, touching nothing but net. Some smack
talking ensues from Mila, as her defender had not
respected her shooting and had double-teamed the pass to
the low post, leaving the shot maker open. Unlike her
male counterparts in Bosnia, this smack talking is done
with a smile, and the beaten defender smiles back and
promises she will not leave her open again, as she raises
her right hand and presses knuckles with Mila.

In the streets of Brooklyn, New York, neighbors gather
to watch mostly young men compete in a basketball game
on cracked asphalt courts on this unusually warm late

winter afternoon. Today's game has a different flavor, as one of the ten participants is Leslie, daughter of Ruben, who is also playing. Leslie is a high school phenom and no one on the court objects to this unique gender exception. Wire fences keep the ball from bouncing to the street but do not prevent local family and friends from entering and taking seats on the rusty three-row bleachers to watch the players, who "should be playing in the NBA." The splendidly talented athletes in their late teens and early twenties (except for Ruben) go at it into the night, with no let up in perspiration or their obsession of putting that leather ball through the bent rims with tattered nets. No matter how late or how long the athletes streak up and down the paved courts, there is always energy left for some special dance after a dunk or some trash talking after a shot rejection in the paint.

Leslie collects a pass from her father at the free throw line, pivots toward the basket and feigns a shot as Jamal leaps high, fully expecting to reject Leslie's shot. Once Jamal is in the air, Leslie takes the dribble to the hoop for an easy lay-up. Ruben high fives his daughter and reminds Jamal that he just got juked by a girl. Making up for his defensive lapse, Jamal takes the ball at the top of the key and drives to the basket, directly at Ruben. Ruben, with a gut matching the weight of the dribbling paint perpetrator, rejects a running one hander. Trotting down the court, Ruben reminds Jamal and his four teammates to keep that "excrement" out of there and turns to the crowd to repeat the banter. Jamal's mother in the third bleacher row will have nothing of it and yells out, even louder than Ruben, a statement of defamation regarding Ruben's lack of prowess off the court. The bleachers break into hearty hysterics; nine players on the court fall to the asphalt, overcome with laughter, followed by Ruben himself. After sixty seconds of levity heard 'round the Brooklyn neighborhood, Ruben, clearly the recognized leader of this basketball community, summons the other nine to their feet and the intense game continues well into the night.

Just outside the small town of Cannelburg, Indiana, four Amish brothers play a two-on-two game in the family barnyard. Cannelburg got its name from a type of coal, cannel coal, discovered a few generations prior to that of these Amish boys, and just a few miles from the barnyard of this hoops engagement. Basketball, farming and coal mining are the three most important aspects of life around Cannelburg—except, of course, God and the Amish religion.

A young twelve-year-old in bibbed overalls and thick brown hair cropped at the ears takes a shot at a rusted goal nailed to the side of the barn. Deciding on a bank shot, he aims for the "I" in the faded "Vikings" painted white on an arch above the rim. The rim is made of a one inch steel band formed into an eighteen inch circle. There is no net attached to the rim but rather a burlap feed bag with a faded Purina logo. An hour earlier, these boys and their dad were hoisting hay bales inside the wall on the other side of the rim; now they play under the Viking emblem that represents the high school they will quit when they reach the age of sixteen. Despite the inevitable interruption of their education required by their Amish culture, they fantasize about being Vikings in their intense game, where the first team to ten baskets wins.

A bearded father with a black, soft felt-brimmed hat coaches one team, wiping his brow while his oldest son Jacob, coaching the other team, yells, "Roll off that pick, Eli! You cain't help the defense no how if ye just let him pick ya still!" Eli vows to watch for the pick next time, as he never wants to disappoint his older brother, the best barnyard basketball player he ever saw. He knew his brother would have been the star of the Vikings if he had stayed in high school for four years. The game is called at nine baskets to nine, when a woman in a white bonnet and white apron over a ground-length plain blue dress comes out to the yard announcing dinner. Intense as this game is, it will be delayed for now and determined later, in deference to Mother's dinner.

It's a Friday night in Atlanta, Georgia; the Atlanta Hawks go head-to-head with their rivals, the Miami Heat. Ten of the best basketball players in the world play on national TV and in front of a sold-out crowd of more than 19,000 people, who make so much noise that the squeaks on the floor cannot be heard. Rabid fans' eyes are adhered to the court below. Some faces are painted in red and black while others wave cards for their beloved Hawks. When a Hawk star guard from the University of Arkansas steals an inbound pass to make a quick jam to build the Hawk's lead, bedlam erupts, deafening all in attendance. The roar pours well beyond the doors and through the packed parking lot surrounding Phillips Arena.

And now, toward the end of this global Friday, in the small northern California town of Los Gatos, Karen and Alasdair, a recently married couple who both work in the Silicon Valley, walk with two out-of-town guests toward downtown. They have a reservation at a superb steakhouse called Forbes Mill. The Silicon Valley couple are native Brits with working visas and their two guests are from Birmingham, England. Strong British accents flow into the evening air as the four of them marvel at the mild evening temperature and the beauty of this quiet, scenic California town.

Los Gatos is a small town that cozies up to the foothills of the Santa Cruz Mountains. It began over a century ago, as the last stop before horse-driven carriages and wagons began the trek over the mountains toward timber mills and the town of Santa Cruz on the Pacific coast. Los Gatos, Spanish for "The Cats," acquired the name from the mountain lions that frequented that same trail the carriages and wagons used. The first business in Los Gatos was the Forbes Mill, along the creek next to the trail. Forbes Mill Steakhouse and the Los Gatos High School Wildcat mascot name are a couple of the few remaining traces of the first settlement. The town has become a wealthy suburb made up of those who succeeded in high technology companies in the adjacent Silicon Valley, and those who succeeded in servicing those who made money in the high-tech companies.

Half a block from the main drag on Bean Avenue, the four pass St. Mary's church and Howley Hall. This hall and small gymnasium serves everything, including St.

Mary's grades kindergarten through eight school plays, the St. Mary's parish country fair spaghetti dinners, bingo, adult and school volleyball games and any other church or school function that needs the space. In this early evening, under the backdrop of the dark-green mountains below a dimming blue sky, the old building's windows emit a yellow glow. As it was time for another St. Mary's paint job; this gymnasium has a slightly worn look. Its somewhat weathered look sticks out, an anomaly in this otherwise perfectly manicured neighborhood. It could have been a gym in Tuzla, Bosnia or Gary, Indiana; but here it stood in a neighborhood in which the average home price is $860,000. This was not your typical universal neighborhood setting for hoops.

Stopping in front of the building, the curious four climb the steps to the double doors facing the street, as they hear what sounds like squeaks accompanied by a pounding sound from inside the gym. To the two Silicon Valley engineers and their friends, these are not familiar sounds, so they slowly open one of the doors an inch or two and peer inside. They see two men with whistles in black-and-white striped shirts running back and forth with ten grade school girls. Blondes, redheads and brunettes with their ponytails and pigtails bobbing up and down were running back and forth ahead of the referees. One girl dribbles the ball at a time, while all ten run back and forth on a wooden floor that needed its annual coating.

Four girls wearing the St. Mary's uniform are yelling, "Carson!" and "Carson, I'm open!" while Carson, determined not to lose the ball to the attacking visiting defenders, dribbles the ball down the floor, eyes fixated on the ball and not her open teammates; her first priority is to protect the ball from the attacking visitors. Carson's team wears yellow shorts and shirts with blue trim and St. Mary's written across their chests just above their numbers.

"Go Cougars!" yells a St. Mary's parent. The Cougar mascot name follows the Los Gatos feline tradition, begun with the high school Wildcats. The opposing team, now gathering around the dribbling Carson, wears bright red shirts and shorts with white trim, and Sacred Heart written in white across the front of their jerseys. When Carson sees Betsy open, she picks up her dribble and makes a bounce pass to her.

That leads to Jordan, Carson, and Betsy's twin brunette sister Meagan yelling, "Betsy!" or, "Betsy, I'm open!"

"Look up! Pass!" yells the St. Mary's volunteer coach, who is also Carson's father.

It is a relatively small gymnasium. The engineers and their guests peer further through the doors; one of the baskets and the baseline reside a mere twelve feet from their position at the doors. They see both teams lined up in a single row of chairs on the right side of the gym narrowly separated by the scorer's bench, run by the St. Mary's athletic director and his son. The feet from both team's benchwarmers rest a mere twelve inches from the out-of-bounds line. Another single row of fold-up seats is on the left side of the gym, mostly fans from the visiting Sacred Heart team from nearby Saratoga. Like the player benches, they're also lined up with twelve inches separating their feet from the out-of-bounds line. More hometown fans are sitting on the stage opposite the entrance doors. The curtains are pulled and some parents sit on the edge of the stage under the far basket. There is a single row of chairs seating additional parents and relatives of the home St. Mary's team behind those hanging their legs off the edge of the stage. Younger brothers and sisters wearing St. Mary's school uniforms of white shirts, blue pants or pleated plaid skirts play dodge ball on the back section of the stage, most of them not as interested in their siblings' game as their parents. Any available space to see the game is taken.

"Stop ball!" yells the Sacred Heart coach. It's a spirited and close game between host St. Mary's Cougars and the Sacred Heart Mustangs. But the absolute beauty of the scene at Howley Hall is that while the squeaks of shoes are fewer and less intense than the whistles, the rules and actions are mostly the same as those of the best in the world playing at the same time in Atlanta, or for that matter earlier in the day in Sudan. You can't dribble again if you pick up the ball. You can only stand in the three-second lane for three seconds. A field goal is two points, a free throw one. Every player on the floor plays offense *and* defense. If everybody is hustling, then all ten players are involved in every single offensive and defensive play. Even those on the bench contribute with warnings about a defensive move, or a "back door" move by a forward on offense. The team that plays as a team and does not try to go "one on five" has a better chance of winning. You get two free throws if a defender fouls you while shooting, etc.

And the fans, mostly family, sitting on the stage or on folding chairs in Howley Hall are every bit as vocal and excited as thousands of Hawks fans in Atlanta.

That's what makes basketball such a beautiful game. While the skill level changes dramatically from fifth-grade girls playing at Howley Hall to that of the Atlanta Hawks and the Miami Heat, the challenge remains the same. How do we put that leather ball through the metal hoop more times than our opponents? And if the many other volunteer youth basketball coaches do their job effectively, like Carson's dad, grade school girls can receive equal or even more emotional rewards than those professionals playing in Atlanta.

*The four British "outsiders" leave the doorway, intrigued by what they saw on the floor at Howley Hall. With a peck on the cheek, the new bride tells Alasdair that if they get citizenship they should consider St. Mary's when they have children. They could spend beautiful Friday nights watching their children playing that game that makes squeaks on the floor, that draws whistles from the guys in the striped shirts and smiles and cheering from those in attendance.*

# 2

## GETTING STARTED

*"We have a great bunch of outside shooters. Unfortunately, all our games are played indoors."*

–Weldon Drew, New Mexico State coach

On my way to coaching young girls in basketball, my first coaching experience was with a group of eighth-grade boys at St. Monica's parish in Creve Coeur, Missouri in 1979. I worked at Monsanto in St. Louis as an engineer right out of college, and a supervisor asked me to coach his son's team. It was a good experience, both comfortable and rewarding. It was about what I expected, having played basketball myself through high school. I was completely at home with a bunch of Midwest boys who were in love with hoops. They were just like me at age thirteen.

It was about that time in St. Louis that I met my wife, which also has a basketball connection. I will never forget what made Dana different, beyond her beauty and brains. She was from Indiana and she spoke basketball.

The first time we sat together at Tully's bar in Creve Coeur, with a Purdue game on the tube, I remember her saying, "That's a moving pick, ref! Come on, his feet were not set!" I looked at her in awe. No Missouri girl I had met knew what a moving pick was. This girl knew hoops! I fell hopelessly in love.

After marriage, my career in robotics took us to Denver, then California. The thought of coaching young kids did not cross my mind for a long time. We had our first daughter, Casey, in California, a second one, Sydney, two years later, and then our bonus baby, Dagney, seven years after Sydney. Having three daughters leads to my first confession. In my single days, when hoops and sports in general were the priority in my life (which is why I stayed single for a long time), I did occasionally let my imagination move forward to marriage and raising a family. Anytime I imagined a family, it was always with boys. Further dreaming included boys who were star athletes and star basketball players. When Dana was carrying our first child, I insisted on naming him Casey. He would be born in the 100th anniversary year of the poem "Casey at the Bat" and I knew that, unlike the mythical Casey, he would *not* strike out. Dana gave birth to a beautiful girl and, we discovered, an athletic one. We stayed with the name Casey. We ended up with no sons and three daughters. Fortunately, I adapted to a house of females, but it was not always easy, as this book recounts—especially for my girls.

When Casey turned four, the prospects of getting her into the excellent private St. Mary's school in our town of Los Gatos looked bleak, given the thriving Silicon Valley economy and the demand for good private schools. Dana reminded me that there were two ways to get Casey into St. Mary's: doing volunteer work, or going the old-fashioned Catholic way and writing a big check. I had not yet made my discovery of the Silicon Valley gold, and the only volunteer skill I felt I had was coaching basketball. I figured the chances of coaching would be slim, given my recollection of volunteer coaches waiting in line in Indiana and the Midwest, not to mention that I was working long hours looking for that gold. My first conclusion was that I needed to sell more robots in the next two years so I could write that check.

Before we get into the details of my first experiences in coaching young girls' basketball, it is relevant for you to know about me. Not that this book is about me, or for that matter any other coach for girls' basketball; the beauty of the story we are going to examine is all about the girls. But for many coaches like me who are highly competitive, it is a huge challenge to put our minds in the proper place for the good of the girls.

I grew up in Indiana in the 60s. My small high school had no girls' sports. Boys had cross-country, baseball, track, and basketball; that was it. I played all the sports I could, but there was never any doubt for me or any other boy that basketball was the pinnacle of high school sports. For small towns in the Midwest in the 1960s, the cultural centerpiece was the high school. In a good way, the town was focused on the students in high school and monitored the progress they made socially and academically in their four years. But above all else was the town's focus on the progress of the high school basketball team. The local team was *their* team, as most, if not all, would be alumni. In Indiana in the 60s and 70s, basketball was not just the national/state pastime, not just a religion, but essentially the reason for getting up in the morning.

My high school was in Montgomery, Indiana, a town of just under 500 residents. Our graduating class totaled 82 students. Yet the basketball gym, with a capacity of two thousand, filled up nearly every game. The parking lot overflowed with cars, pickup trucks, and horses and carriages of the local Amish, hitched to light posts or swing sets after braving cold and snowy rides from the countryside. On any given night in southwestern Indiana during the basketball season, if a fan's school did not have a game, he/she went to the closest town that did have a game.

I can still remember taking in the home crowd on the filled lower level during pre-game lay-ups, seeing the cheer block in one corner displaying a black V formed by those in black shirts surrounded by white shirts. Two blocks of seats over, I would see more of the Viking black and white, this time the habits of the Benedictine nuns from the local St. Peter's grade school. Next to them would be the white bonnets of the Amish women intermixed with the bright, single-colored shirts of their male counterparts, complete with suspenders and brimmed hats. On the opposite side of the floor would be the opposing cheer block, chanting with the guidance of their cheerleaders and a huge number of out-of-town students and visitors. The upper deck would be jammed with more local and visiting high school fans, along with players and coaches from other teams who did not have a game that night. All four double-door entranceways would be packed with standing-room-only fans, certainly an emergency hazard.

I would submit that high school basketball was the cultural center of every small town in southern Indiana in my time. The coach's office was the rectory and the gymnasium was the temple of the high school. The entrance lobby to most Indiana high school gyms contained a glass-front locked trophy case of past victories; my high school was no exception. We also had framed pictures of decades of past teams hanging in the hallways around the gym. Teams that won state sectionals and regionals had larger pictures, and those in the pictures were legends. What made the wins even more special at my high school was that in those days, the Indiana system did not separate schools by size into different divisions. When our high school of three hundred beat schools with enrollments of thousands, it was a big deal; it was part of our proud history. Individual and team records were recorded on the inner walls, the walls that got fresh paint every year, while the study hall might get a paint job every six years. Every year the floor of the gym was stripped, repainted, coated and varnished to a glistening shine, and the Viking symbol with the two big horns at the centerline repainted as well. If any student was caught on the floor in something other than Converse shoes or socks, it was study hall detention. I remember classmate Tony taking a shortcut in his street shoes across the far corner of our gym floor after a basketball pep rally, barely in bounds. Our junior varsity coach grabbed him by the collar and dragged him to study hall, where he served time for two weeks. He was warned that a second offense could mean suspension.

You can imagine how our religion reached the highest peak when my high school's Blue Chip Conference produced Larry Bird of Springs Valley at French Lick. If you were lucky to make it to varsity you were the big duck in the small pond in the town of Montgomery, or any other small town in the hills of southern Indiana. The boy from French Lick was that one guy who became the giant among giants, the new Indiana state "Bird". (And speaking of French Lick, I've always liked what a comedian once said about Indiana in the 60s: North Vernon was in southern Indiana, South Bend was in Northern Indiana, and French Lick was also not what he expected.)

Even in the poor coal mining and farming community of Montgomery in the 60s and 70s, there were perks for the high school hoops players. Before high school basketball, I desperately scrambled for any summer job I could get. For $.75 or $1 an hour I pulled weeds from the rows of cornfields, then later in the year cut tassels from the tops of the cornstalks. In the eighth grade I moved up to chicken and turkey catching for $1.25 an hour. Five or six of us cheap and unskilled laborers would form a line, yelling and waving our hands to herd the flustered fowl into a fenced area. We would then grab the startled birds, a leg between each finger, and stuff them into crates. After stuffing, we would shake the excrement off our hands, grab another three per hand and repeat. If you were lucky, you could get a "de-beaking" project assignment. In this job we would herd young chicks into a similarly wired pen. This time we picked up one chick at a time, pressed an index finger into the side of the beak to separate, placed the upper beak on a flat plate on the "de-beaker," pressed the foot pedal, and the hot blade would sever the upper beak, producing a small screech and a smell not unlike that one senses getting a filling in the dentist's chair. We would then drop the de-beaked young fowl across the fence, shake a smaller amount of excrement off our hands (you would produce that too, if you were the chick) and grab the next unsuspecting victim.

After making the junior varsity basketball team, I got a better job loading and unloading fertilizer trucks for local

fertilizer magnate Joe Traylor, a huge Viking fan and sup-
porter. Later on an even better summer job appeared, and
I drove the same truck to Amish homes and unloaded
twenty-four-inch ice blocks into the underground cellars
where the Amish (whose religion did not allow 20th century luxuries like electricity) stored their dairy products,
meat and other fresh foods. After making varsity, I got the
plush job of lifeguarding at the local lake, run by the high
school athletic director. I call this a perk, because any job
was hard to come by in the poor country towns in
southern Indiana in the 60s. Besides holding a summer
job, we were expected to work out at the gym in the mornings or evenings without coaches, who were not allowed
to participate in organized basketball activity with the
players until October 1.

My all-time favorite movie is *Hoosiers*, and not solely
because the drama is based on a real small southern
Indiana high school team (Milan High School, led by
Bobby Plump in 1954) that won the state championship.
The incredible accomplishment for Milan was that the
town had a population of 1150 and the high school had
only 161 students, yet the Milan Indians won the state
championship against large city teams in those days of the
single division Indiana system. They won the championship 32 to 30 against the large perennial power school
Muncie Central, with Bobby Plump freezing the ball for
four minutes in the fourth quarter against the much taller
Bearcats, then hitting a fourteen footer to clinch the two-
point win at the buzzer. The movie *Hoosiers* also accurately portrayed the way small Indiana towns lived and

died with their high school team. (I cry each time I see the movie.) I embarrassed Dana once at a Los Gatos dinner party when we were going around the table citing our top three movies of all time. The woman prior to me named movies in foreign languages, mostly French, which I did not recognize. When it was my turn, I cited *Caddyshack*, *Rudy*, and *Hoosiers* as #1. When the lady with the foreign accent asked what *Hoosiers* was about and I began my summary, I found my eyes welling with tears the way they do every time I watch the film (twenty-three and counting). Dana quickly changed the subject and I excused myself to the restroom to regain my composure.

I am not the only Hoosier who adores this movie. Last year I made a trip to Washington, D.C. with Mayor Cris Ockomon of Anderson, Indiana to discuss government support for a factory I wanted to place in Anderson. I saw two full-size *Hoosier* movie posters in the offices of Indiana-elected politicians Congressman Mike Pence and Senator Richard Lugar. Congressman Pence's poster was signed by Bobby Plump, the star of that Milan team. I got goose bumps and carried them with me as I entered their offices for our meeting. It created a wonderful bond. They adored Indiana's basketball history, just like me. Congressman Pence went to Indiana University, a bitter rival of Purdue, and I had to get that out of the way early in our meeting. Both of us being from southern Indiana and loving basketball made for a warm one-hour session. My colleagues and I even received a personal tour of the Capital from Congressman Pence. No Boilermakers vs. Hoosiers, Hatfields vs. McCoys in southern Indiana, because we bond with our hoops.

I have always been obsessed with sports. Even now, when I am out of town on business and don't hear Steve Bitker's morning sports report on KCBS radio, or don't read San Jose Mercury News sportswriter Mark Purdy in the morning, I feel a certain imbalance going into my business meetings.

I inherited my father's love for sports. While he was a basketball player and a good athlete, I lost him in a coal mining accident when I was two, so I discovered my passion for sports and basketball on my own. I grew up with the incredible fostering of an amazing widowed mother who worked in a munitions factory, and two sisters who had no opportunity to play sports. I also inherited my father's competitiveness, almost to a fault. From the time I was a young boy, *everything* was a competition: my grades versus my sisters', racing with my dog, getting to the front of the line for recess at school, picking the winners in the Indianapolis 500, the St. Peter's spelling bee ... If the Evansville Diocese had an All-Diocese altar boys'squad, I would have fully expected to make first team, since I was always picked to serve for special Holy Week services and weddings. I spoke the Latin mass frontward and backward, rang the bells with a consistent if not melodious tone, and no one tossed the incense better than I did (in my mind, of course).

I did not limit myself to basketball but played every sport I could, depending on the season. Despite excruciating pain in my lungs, I even ran cross-country. After all, it was a race—and races are meant to be won. Before every Little League baseball game I would make my sister Clara throw me pitches in the back yard while sister Brenda shagged the balls. One night I drilled Clara's fastball into her chest. After I saw she was breathing, I let her rest on the ground in foul territory and asked Brenda to take over pitching—and to throw the next pitches more inside so I could pull the ball. Looking back, it was pathetic. Looking back with embarrassment is part of the aging and mellowing process, and though even today I have not reached the full 100% mellow state, I am close.

In some ways, I became even more competitive as a coach than as a player—or, for that matter, a robot salesman. This may have been fed by the fact that two broken arms and a knee injury limited my quest for sports beyond high school. One of the first girls' games I ever coached was Sydney's third/fourth-grade team, the Heat, in the Los Gatos Recreational League. "The Rec" was an excellent league that is all about kids learning the game and getting equal playing time. As such, each team of ten played five girls every other quarter, so no substitutions could be made until the end of the quarters.

In the fourth quarter we were leading the Lakers by one point with about a minute to go. At this age, being up 11-10 was a reasonably good position to be in with a minute left. The other team had the ball and one of their girls suddenly went down on one knee to tie her shoelace. When the opposing Laker coach saw she could not play because of unplanned shoe maintenance, he pushed another girl onto the court to take her place and yelled for the shoelace girl to come to the sideline. Now, unnoticed by the young referees, he had a new (illegally substituted) girl whom none of my girls were assigned to guard. As luck would have it, she got the ball—unguarded, as my defensive girl followed the shoelace girl to her bench. All alone, she dribbled closer to the basket and made a wide open shot to take the lead, 12-11.

"She was an illegal substitution!" I screamed after she scored.

But the refs were young, timid high-school kids who barely knew the game and clearly had not seen the illegal substitution. Suddenly realizing I was screaming at innocent young teenagers, I pulled myself back and buttoned my lip, flaming on the inside as the clock ran out with no further scoring. I was so mad I did not allow myself to open my mouth as I shook the hand of the opposing (cheating) coach, not wanting to further embarrass my daughter or Dana.

But it did not end there. I sulked the whole weekend, and the next weekend. Two years later I woke up in the middle of the night, saying, "She was an illegal substitution." Four years later, I began spotting that Lakers' coach at St. Mary's masses, a few pews in front of me. I have to confess I actually fantasized about working my way to a seat next to him so that during the mass's "sign of peace" handshake I could once again shake his hand, smile and say, "Peace be with you, even though you illegally substituted number three and stole that game from us in 1998."

I got my family to go to mass at a different time, to help me deal with my problem. It was about then that I came to the realization that I had an illness, which I dubbed Overly Competitive Coaching Disorder (OCCD). It infects men and women who exhibited highly competitive personalities in their youth and then the effect compounds when their athletic skills deteriorate in later years. It only gets worse when the ex-jock chooses to feed his/her addiction through a new drug, coaching. It is a sickness, and I took the first big step by admitting my affliction.

Since that time I have had a few incidents in games where I relapsed to my sickened state. But most of the time when temptation struck, I was able to stop myself and gather my composure by uttering "OCCD!" to myself. Similar to the *Seinfeld* episode in which Frank Costanza calms himself by yelling "Serenity Now!" I had to chant to myself in order to keep from making a fool of myself.

I saw the Lakers coach again in a deli line during a work lunch in the Valley recently. Though both of our daughters from that game are now in college I wondered if I might introduce myself as a former fellow coach, ask where his daughter went to college, and maybe share a laugh to point out his bold indiscretion during that game. He probably would not remember me and certainly would not remember the game. Could this be latent OCCD rearing its ugly head? I closed my eyes, took a deep breath, reminded myself about my OCCD and ordered my pastrami. I had not had an OCCD relapse for quite some time, but the incident served as a wakeup call that while you can beat OCCD, it is a permanent disorder, and I will always be tested with temptations.

I confess this competitive illness to make the point that I was/am part of that cross section of grown "has-been" male (or female) athletes who are past their prime and think they can fulfill that competitive drive by coaching young kids. With this background, this book can address the critical aspect of balancing the coach's competitiveness with the girls' basketball experience.

Going back to one night in 1993, after a long day at the robot factory, Dana brought up the topic of volunteering at St. Mary's. Enrollment demand was well over supply at St. Mary's, and folks who made contributions might get the first look. Since robots were the technology of the future (and would always remain so), there were not a lot of dollars in the coffer to contribute. She felt that volunteerism was almost as good as contributions, and I told her that I totally supported *her* volunteering at St. Mary's. That was when I got the look that told me she already had a volunteer plan that went beyond her own time.

"St. Mary's has boys' and girls' teams from grades five to eight. They might need coaches and assistant coaches," she pointed out. "You played hoops and coached boys in St. Louis."

"But Dana, even if there was an opening, I am trying to make this startup robot company work, and it's long hours plus lots of travel …"

"The seventh- and eighth-grade boys and girls practice late and play the late games. You can get one of your application engineers, maybe Steve, to be your assistant when you are traveling …" It was not a debate that I was going to win. I had to admit that my competitive side needed fulfillment, now that my aching knees no longer allowed me to dunk in my club games and I was trying to improve my three-point shot to compensate.

Since getting our daughter into St. Mary's was the big challenge, I put a lot of thought into the résumé I would respectfully submit to Sister Nicki, principal at St. Mary's. Assuming there were many fathers or mothers who would love to coach and/or want to get their child into St. Mary's with whom I would be competing for the job got my competitive juices flowing as I put my qualifications down on paper. I was worried they would find out that I had not made it at Purdue hoops, so I added our winning record when coaching the boys' team and emphasized my high school accomplishments, including varsity basketball co-captain ... and even my MVP and Mental Attitude awards.

I stopped just short of All-Around Nice Guy who loves sunsets and walks on the beach. I sent the résumé to Sister Nicki and anxiously awaited her response. The response from Sister Nicki was my first hint that this was not Indiana—and that California basketball was culturally a distant follower to other sports and activities. "Ah, just call Dave, our Athletic Director, and you don't need to send him your résumé." I found out later that I was the only one in the history of St. Mary's coach volunteers to send a résumé. I also learned that Dave Freitas was an amazing Athletic Director/substitute coach/substitute ref/clock keeper/floor sweeper ... (I disovered later that every Catholic grade school in the St. Mary's league had a "Dave

Freitas" which collectively made the backbone of a successful grade school sports program.)

Thirty seconds into a phone call with Dave that I
assumed was to set up an interview, he said, "Yeah, we
can't find anyone to coach the seventh-grade boys' team, if
you wanna take a shot at it." That was it: one hour on a
résumé that was never read, half a minute on the phone,
and I was volunteering my daughter's way into St. Mary's.
Turns out, they were beyond desperate for someone who
knew hoops; they were desperate for a body with a pulse. I
was not in Indiana anymore, and not even Kansas.

While basketball was not a top priority for Sister Nicki
(she had this hang-up about the quality of education being
top priority), I will always remember the first coaches'
meeting and the words of Dave Najour, Chairman of the
St. Mary's Athletic Board, during a policy discussion on
fair playing time for all kids, regardless of talent.

"Just remember one thing. In this world of competitive
high school sports, St. Mary's basketball will be both the
first and the last school basketball experience for most, if
not all, of these kids. Make it a great memory for them."
Dave's words are the best advice a competitive coach like
me could have gotten. While it has not been easy, given
my intense competitiveness, I have lived by those words at
St. Mary's and even while coaching highly competitive
National Junior Basketball club teams.

When I saw my boys warming up on the first day of
practice, Dave's words rang true, as clearly none of these
boys would be playing Division I or even high school basketball. I remember the look I got from young Scott when

I said, "Each night, when you are home practicing your jump shots in your driveway or neighborhood court, take a few extra minutes to work on your weak hand …" I asked Scott what was wrong. After some back and forth, I realized that the *only* time these boys would touch a basketball was at St. Mary's practices and games, due to conflicts with volleyball, scouting, guitar lessons, academic clubs, chess clubs, social clubs …

This was culture shock. Growing up in Indiana, I shot hoops seven days a week starting in the first grade. I did it because I loved it and it was free. I shot on the asphalt courts, the hoops on neighborhood garages, in my back yard at the hoop on a telephone pole, in barnyards, and, when I was lucky, in the gym. At a later age, I had access to two different gyms at my high school, and joined the other "gym rats" who played basketball seven days a week. Winter Saturday mornings, when the outdoor courts were covered in snow, I would wait in the cold with my fellow grade school pals in front of the high school doors at 8 a.m. for the school janitor to open the doors. We would play until he ran us out, well into the afternoon. When the gyms were unavailable, I remember playing three on threes in the bitter cold, dribbling on asphalt courts or in barnyards on frozen hoof prints that could career a ball wildly. That environment was very conducive to a passing game in lieu of dribbling past defenders.

It was that "gym rat" passion that carried all the way through my high school team and that I have not seen since, especially in California. Even the basketball uniform numbering scheme was flawed with the California teams I coached. Everybody (at least any Hoosier) knows that any basketball jersey number can never be more than 5 for a single digit or 5 for either of the two-digit numbers. This allows the referee to assign a foul to a player with one hand, signaling up to five fingers once or twice while holding the whistle or ball in the other hand. I was surprised to find number 68 and number 99 in the jersey pile at St. Mary's. I had to accept the Los Gatos "If this is Tuesday it must be volleyball" mindset. Later, I came to realize how lucky these kids were to experience multiple sports and other cultural activities. I also realized that one of the most important challenges of getting started was setting priorities in a non-basketball culture. We will cover more on that in the next chapter.

Despite hoops being a lower priority, my St. Mary's boys' team had winning seasons in both the seventh grade and eighth grade years, and I ended the second season looking forward to coaching Casey when she became old enough to play.

In fact, my first real indoctrination to the culture of girls'basketball came the year of coaching Casey on the St. Mary's fifth-grade girls' team and my Sydney on the Heat, a Los Gatos girls' recreational team. Casey had played as a third and fourth grader in the Recreational League and had established herself as one of the best in this modestly competitive league. I had been traveling extensively for business during those two years and was not able to coach her much nor expose her to the National Junior Basketball (NJB) league. Casey was very aggressive and absolutely loved basketball. I asked her early in the fifth-grade school year if her classmates liked to play sports like she did.

When she said, "Yeah, I think so, and Caitlin played NJB last year," I was already fantasizing about coaching a group of good, highly motivated fifth-grade athletes like Casey and Caitlin. I will always remember that first afternoon in Howley Hall with nine St. Mary's fifth-grade Cougars sitting on the stage as I stood before them for the first time. I briefly thought back to my days as a player and the initial meetings with high school coaches at the beginning of each season. Then, I clung to every word they said and tried to memorize each message, each tip. I did not want to miss a single detail to ensure my good standing and to maximize my playing time. In my first introductory speech from Joe Todrank at Barr Reeve High School, Coach said he would take out any player bent over on the free throw line with hands on knees trying to catch his breath. I made a mental note about free throw posture and being in shape, and then ran the steps in the gym after practice while the rest of my teammates showered. I knew the potential importance of the first coach speech that I was about to make to my team.

"Hello girls, I am Mr. Duncheon, Casey's dad. I will be your coach this year. You can call me Coach or Coach Charlie. We will be focusing mostly on fundamentals ..." There were two Caitlins on the team. Caitlin #1 (no particular order) was the daughter of my friend and assistant coach, Paul. As I continued speaking, I was ignoring Caitlin #2, the NJB player with basketball genes, who was enthusiastically raising her right hand, pumping it upward with her left hand clutching the elbow. "We will start from the beginning playing man-to-man defense ... err. I mean girl-on-girl ... err. I mean girl-to-girl defense."

Caitlin #2 was about to throw her right arm out of the socket, supporting it in upward thrusts with her left hand, mumbling, "Mmm! Mmm! Mmm!" I really wanted to get through my introduction speech, but she was becoming a distraction to the rest of the girls.

"Yes, Caitlin, you have a question?" I relented.

"Yes I do, coach. Where are we going to have our end-of-year party?"

"I vote for Mountain Mike's," volunteered Andrea.

"If it is warm we could go to Raging Waters," added Brittnay. I stood silent, rendered speechless. (For the record, Caitlin indeed exhibited excellent hoop skills, despite it not being her first priority.)

Random thoughts from nowhere became a familiar pattern that year with my St. Mary's fifth grade, Calvary League, NJB, and Los Gatos Recreational League teams. I will share some of those stories as we go along; there was no limitation to the time and place of their occurrences, even during time-precious timeouts. One of the more memorable comments from a player came at the end-of-year party that Caitlin so looked forward to that same season. It was at a pizza place, and once again I stood in front of the fifth-grade girls, this time presenting each girl with a memento and describing her best feat of the season. Proud (I think) parents stood behind the table of girls and I was inspired to give one last motivational speech for both the girls and the parents. We won six and lost five that year and it was the closest I would ever come to a losing season. I decided to dissect the game into individual components and speak about why each component of teamwork is necessary for a winning season.

"Girls, remember the St. Frances Cabrini game?" I asked. "What do you remember most about that game?" (We won by one point with a winning basket in the last thirty seconds.)

Janelle, with another dislodging-arm-socket hand raise, answered, "Number 17 getting hit in the face by Andrea and then crying on the bench."

Not what I was looking for, so I responded, "Actually, I had in mind that we beat Cabrini by one point. But it was not only Casey's winning basket with thirty seconds to go that I will remember. I will remember Kelsey forcing the bad shot with her good defense. If she had not forced the bad shot, Christina would not have gotten that great rebound. And if Christina had not gotten that great rebound, Caitlin would not have had a reason to break to the outside for the outlet pass. And if Caitlin had not broken to the outside lane to get Christina's pass, she would not have been able to take the two dribbles and pass to Casey streaking down the other lane. And if Caitlin had not made that great pass, Casey would not have been able to hit the lay-up to win the game. It took the team-work of four girls to ensure that one-point victory AND to make sure we had a winning 6-5 season. You see, team-work ... " Another hand pumping toward the sky, this one by the dark eyed, dark-haired and usually low key Amanda, who had not been part of the teamwork sequence I had just described. Allowing the interruption just prior to my rehearsed dramatic climax, I sighed, "Yes, Amanda."

Looking around at her teammates to gather full attention, Amanda calmly pointed out, "If that blonde girl on Cabrini had not gotten mixed up and scored that basket at *our* goal, we would not have had a winning season," and then took another bite of her pepperoni pizza.

"Thanks for sharing that, Amanda. Everybody enjoy the pizza and I look forward to next year," were the only words I could muster.

Given St. Mary's ethic that each student gets fair playing time, we usually had two teams per class for both boys and girls. This meant tryouts in front of the two coaches, and then the coaches would draft their players one at a time. We had a similar process at the NJB level in Los Gatos, where we might have as many as three coaches drafting for three ten-player club teams. This would only happen after the NJB All Net coach chose his/her top ten players from the pool for the advanced All Net league. In my personal experience, both the St. Mary's and NJB drafts were conducted at the local Irish Pub, CB Hannegan's. (Now that I think about it, I pushed for that venue.) While they did not have the flash of the ESPN pro drafts, we had lots of smack talking as we kept one eye on the chart on the table and the other on the notes in our laps.

The temptation at the young age is to look for height; after all, basketball is a game for giants, right? But I learned that height can mean very little at the inexperienced grade school level. In the NJB fourth-grade All Star Nationals, my team was shorter than every team we faced. We came in second in the Nationals because our team was led by three excellent ball-handling guards. All my girls had better-than-average speed, and they were simply better athletes. Besides, taller girls or boys who grow earlier in life have coordination challenges as they are constantly adapting to their changing body dimensions; the hoop keeps changing its angle to their eyes in shooting. In later years you pay the piper for height, and all the other basketball skills—but in the early years, guards and good athletes will beat tall girls who are adapting to their changing bodies.

Anyway, the drafts are fun for coaches like me, who would rather be coaching full time than selling expensive robots. One thing is for sure–each coach leaves these drafts thinking that he/she was a better judge of talent than the opposing coaches, and made the best drafts. The adult beverages probably contribute to that perspective, which is disproved for most of us during the regular season.

# 3

## PRIORITIES

*"Son, looks to me like you're spending too much time on one subject."*

–Shelby Metcalf, basketball coach at Texas A&M, to a player who received four F's and one D

On January 13, 2009, the girls' varsity basketball team of Covenant High School in Dallas, Texas beat the girls' team from Dallas Academy 100-0. Beyond the lopsided score, the Covenant team finished with a flurry of three-point shots, Covenant parents went into frenzy as they approached 100.[1] To its credit, following coverage in the Dallas Morning News, the Covenant School posted a communication on its website the next day, saying "It is shameful and an embarrassment that this happened." The following Sunday, the Covenant coach made a public statement on a basketball website defending his actions in the 100-0 game. Shortly after, Covenant High School fired him.

When I read this in the *San Jose Mercury News*, all I could think about were the girls on the Dallas Academy team and the pain their parents must have gone through. There are those who would argue that by high school, kids need to get ready for the real world, and winning teams should not let up in such a game. But I will take the odds and say that none of the girls on the Covenant team will be playing WNBA hoops. Their claim to fame will be a 100-0 shutout instead of showing compassion and leadership, traits they will need when they graduate and enter the non-basketball world.

But of course it was not the fault of the girls; in my opinion, it was that of their coach. I have already mentioned my difficulty with culture shock in California. Eventually, I realized that my cultural surprise and frustration were based on my motivation as a coach to win. It was not easy at first but in later years I was able to motivate myself by focusing on positive player development and experience, but it was not easy in the early years of coaching.

In discussing priorities for young girls' basketball, I think it is important to break each sector into levels of seriousness. I will list the fifth-grade levels, at least in the local area where I have coached, by level of seriousness and commitment.

Grade School Basketball – There are exceptions, but in general this is the least competitive level, and coaches have to accept the lowest priority given to basketball, both by the girls and their parents. At the fifth- and sixth-grade level, the girls cannot be guarded in the backcourt and free throws are shot a couple feet in front of the standard line. Fair, if not equal, playing time is required for all players. One thing that I will say about school basketball: The spirit and emotion is the highest of all other levels of club basketball. In my experience with Casey, that enthusiastic spirit for the game continued through high school. I also saw it with her field hockey, even compared to college-level games. There was just no comparison between the spirit and support in the stands of an Archbishop Mitty High School field hockey game vs. her Northeastern Division I field hockey games.

Recreational Basketball – Los Gatos has the city Recreational League and the Calvary Church leagues that offer hoops at the earliest ages. Both leagues depend heavily on volunteers, and the Calvary League mixes in good spiritual training. Strict equal playing time rules apply to both leagues.

National Junior Basketball (NJB) Division Basketball – The NJB is club basketball, the next level up from the recreational leagues, with paid staff. Los Gatos typically would have multiple teams per age/gender group. Equal playing time is required for the first four periods, and then a fifth period is played with no substitution requirements. The top "All Star" NJB teams come from several states at the end of the year to Anaheim, California for the NJB National Tournaments. In my opinion, Division NJB is an outstanding venue, balancing competitiveness, development and positive experiences.

NJB All Net and AAU– The highest level of girls' basketball is the upper echelon of NJB, All Net. Tryouts occur at the start of the season. If there are enough good players, Los Gatos might have one All Net team per age/ gender group, and those who are cut are guaranteed to play division. High school rules apply and there are no substitution policies. My experience in coaching against American Athletic Union (AAU) girls' basketball club teams with my All Net teams show strong parity, as we have a slight winning edge against them. But by the time the girls reach eighth grade and beyond AAU is the highest level of competition.

One thing I have always admired about the NJB program is the lower costs that allow more kids to play. With the heavy volunteer efforts of parents in coaching and administrating, the season can cost a few hundred dollars for a kid to play versus thousands of dollars for other sports like club volleyball.

I submit that for coaches, the priority cannot be the enhancement of the coach's winning percentage for consideration at higher levels of coaching. (Though my next confession is that as recently as three years ago, I knew my overall youth coaching career record.) Coaching fifth-grade girls' basketball must have not only the goal of winning games but also goals to improve skills, teach teamwork, make new friends, win and lose with grace, and balance basketball with other important young girl activities. Though we competitive coaches don't like it, we have to accept that there are legitimate conflicts to practices and games. Those conflicts go beyond other sports; if a player has fallen behind in class, homework must have priority over practice. Certain family events will always have priority over hoops. Again, we are talking about young girls.

Winning versus longer term player development can be in conflict with internal team priorities. This priority conflict can surface with the "tall early" girls (or boys) in basketball (or volleyball). The temptation for coaches is to play the tall girls under the basket at forward or center positions. I have seen tall and very athletic girls dominate the game under the baskets in their early years and then stop growing by the seventh grade. By the time they get to high school they are not tall enough to play the forward positions. At the same time, they did not get the ball handling and passing experiences at the guard positions. The "tall early" girls can hit a dead end if their coaches' priority was winning first and development second. My advice to coaches is to take a look at the parents of their "tall early" girls. If they are not tall, mix in some point guard and shooting guard experience for their daughters.

Winning *is* a priority, but not at the expense of humiliating the losing ten-year-old girls. The NJB is wonderfully focused around the experience of young kids and has excellent mercy rules to avoid this, even at their highest All Net level. If you are not coaching within mercy rules, you can always make moves like unloading your bench, dropping to a non-pressing zone or requiring four passes before shooting. None of these moves lessens the winning team's "development," which is the tired excuse of the bully coach. I can relate to the motives of adult coaches to win in this age group, but have never understood the motive to win BIG, especially since I have been on the bench during such a pummeling and have had to deal with the emotions and self-esteem of my girls, who lost big. With three daughters, I have learned much about the fragility of self-esteem at this young age. We do not need to compound that problem with a humiliating pounding on the basketball court.

It took me some time, but I realized in my Los Gatos/ St. Mary's coaching experience that no one in this town was taking basketball as seriously as I was. I learned that all of us coaches must not take it personally when our young kids lose. It was not easy for me in the initial years, but eventually I realized that good coaches are made by good players. You can't take it personally when you lose with less talented players than your opposition. Whitey Herzog, manager of the St. Louis Cardinals baseball team, said it best when he lost his ace reliever, Bruce Sutter, to the Atlanta Braves in free agency. "I just got 45 games dumber."

So both the players' talents and their priorities set boundaries on a coach's expectations. I heard a story from Caitlin #2's father about when her uncle came to town for a visit. Caitlin's father was an excellent basketball player, having played Division I, and his brother had his own rich athletic history. The animated uncle's conversation with his niece Caitlin went something like this.

"So Caitlin, did I hear you are playing basketball?"

"Yes."

"I'm so excited about that, what is the name of your team?"

"The Cougars. It's my St. Mary's school team."

"What position are you playing?"

"Coach plays me at four and five."

"Are you having a good year?"

"I guess."

"Are you scoring, blocking shots and getting rebounds?" Uncle is really getting into his niece's exploits at this point.

"Yes."

"So what is it that you like to do the most?"

"Shopping," she responded, with the same beautiful, beaming smile she had at the start of the conversation.

I was glad Caitlin's dad shared the story with me; it not only reminded me of the priorities in fifth-grade girls' minds, but also of how far I was removed from that mindset. I again realized that Caitlin (and probably most of her teammates) did not share my priority for winning, despite her being a very good athlete. The incident challenged me to somehow make basketball practice more fun than shopping.

I learned that there are priorities that have to be addressed for hoops at this age, within reasonable limits. You can have the priority to win, but within a good balance with the experience. One priority that must be met regards grooming. With girls, you have to insist on pigtails, ponytails or braids. The NJB has a good grooming rule: no jewelry or "metal" on the players. I liked this rule. What California culture viewed as jewelry, I saw as "shrapnel" on young girls, showing up on ears, noses and other parts of their anatomy. This grooming issue becomes a priority issue around the seventh grade, especially when seventh-grade boys are on the sidelines waiting for their practice or game.

In the sixth grade Sydney, who was always a good shooter (and never saw a shot she didn't like, according to certain teammates) suddenly went into a shooting slump. I watched her for three straight games and could not figure out what she was doing differently. (I could only analyze her in games, as she was not inclined to shoot in the driveway with me.) Then, at one of our practices, I noticed that her shot had a lower arc and no backspin. Moving closer, I noted a clicking sound as she was shooting in the shoot around. Looking even closer I suddenly saw the change: the long, purple fingernails she was suddenly brandishing. She could not release the ball with backspin with those long nails, and instead was "dispensing" her shot. Amid much protest, I cut them on the spot, and by the end of practice she was knocking them down again. I was so happy with solving the mystery that I decided to institute a fingernail inspection process that I still use today.

My pride in solving the flat shot mystery was somewhat diminished a year later when the same normally timid Sydney grabbed me by the shoulders on the seventh grade practice court, looked me in the eyes sternly, glaring under her perfectly brushed blond hair, and said, "Dad, read my lips. I don't ever want to play basketball again. I hate sports! The only reason I ever played was 'cause you made me!"

I was shattered, and all I could respond with was, "But Sydney, we haven't lost a game yet at St. Mary's and if you quit, there are other dads who should coach ... and ..."

Then I realized my sin. My priority for Sydney was for her to be a similar star athlete like her older sister Casey, for my joy in coaching her. Her timidity allowed me to set those priorities when she would rather be doing something else. It wasn't as if I did not have a few clues from my diffident Sydney along the way. We had to remind her to take her uniform to school and actually show up on time for the game. I remember one time, as the buzzer rang for the tipoff at St. Mary's sixth grade opening game against St. Lucy's, realizing that Sydney, my starting shooting guard, was one block away at the Kid in a Candystore shop with teammate Lauren.

Later that night in our living room, with the intervention of the smarter of the two parents, her mother and Sydney agreed that she could quit hoops, soccer and other sports as long as she took up another activity. She agreed, and in one year was the lead singer and guitar player in a band and was acting and singing in musicals for a children's musical theater. I could not take credit for that one, but I learned an important lesson about priorities, more as a parent than a coach. And the truth is, when I saw her singing as Mrs. Walker in *Tommy* her senior year at Archbishop Mitty High School, I got goose-bumps that I never got watching Casey hit her first three-pointer. Nothing could move me more than watching a daughter accomplish something I could never do, and singing the lead in *Tommy* was one of many of Sydney's examples of that.

So priorities are not only important for the coach, but also for the parents. It is usually dads who need grounding on priorities for their girls (and boys), but even mothers can get caught up in the obsession of the Division I scholarship. I saw this obsession gain momentum with parents of daughters with the passage of Title 9, which required universities to meet gender equality standards in awarding athletic scholarships to student athletes. It is especially prevalent with fathers like me, who didn't have sons. I recall Monday morning coffee at my desk with a coworker who had returned from his eighth-grade daughter's volleyball tournament in Atlanta. She had a great tournament, and despite the jet lag, he was clearly charged about the prospects of a full ride volleyball scholarship for his daughter.

"How much did the weekend cost you?" I asked him.

"Wasn't cheap, twenty-four hundred for our round-trip tickets."

"How about hotel?"

"I dunno, maybe four-hundred."

"Meals?"

"Maybe two-hundred bucks. No wait, the dads went out Saturday night afterwards, probably four-hundred."

"And how many of these have you done this year?"

"Well, I guess this is the fifth out-of-town tournament."

"And how much are the volleyball team dues?"

"Four thousand a year."

"How many years has she been doing this with the club?"

"Well, this is the fourth year of the traveling team. Why are you asking?" Banging on my desk calculator, I showed him that he had already paid for a four-year degree in the California University system—and he still had four years of club volleyball to go before college. If he was not over jet lag before, he was then.

The point is that your daughter or son should play a sport for the love of it, not for that elusive full ride scholarship that so few kids get anyway. In recent years those scholarships have become even more elusive, as college men's and women's teams recruit athletes from all over the globe. Attending one of Casey's college field hockey games, I did a count on the roster of both teams, Northeastern vs. Hofstra; about half the players were international students. And other statistics I've seen spell out the scholarship challenge. Out of 330,000 high school football seniors 10,000 will get financial aid to play in college. And only 1.8% of high school soccer players will play in college. The numbers are just another reminder to coaches that when push comes to shove academics and homework must always have priority over his/her team practices.

Maybe Sydney saved me club basketball dollars with her sudden proclamation. All things considered, I still would submit that basketball is better for young girls than performing arts. Take cuts, for example. Nothing has been more painful for me as a coach than to have to inform a ten-year-old girl who did not make my final ten for All Net. It rips me apart. One parent advised that I should always call the girl directly, and that was good advice. Over time, I realized that it was more important for a girl with a deep passion for the game to make the team, over a natural athlete who did not have the passion. I came to admire Casey's high school field hockey coach, Justina Williams, especially the way she handled cuts from her championship teams. She would take the girl into her office, give her the bad news, and then would end up with more tears than the girl who did not make the team. It is not unlike the good corporate manager in business having to lay off a good employee.

Theater, on the other hand, seems not so subtle or sensitive regarding cuts. I remember Sydney singing her heart out at tryouts for a children's theater in San Jose, then losing sleep for two nights in anticipation of getting her first lead part. On cast announcement day, the theater simply announced the parts online and Sydney, like everyone else, read that she did not get a lead part. In high school, she might read that she did not get any part at all. No meetings in the office, no phone calls.

Once she got the guts to call the artistic director to inquire why she was not chosen, only to get a curt and succinct response, "Because you had a lousy audition." Performing arts is harsh on young girls. One positive for Sydney was that Archbishop Mitty High School, which has a reputation as perhaps the best performing arts high school in the Bay Area, seemed to tilt in the favor of juniors and seniors who stuck it out for the full four high school years. I saw no such pattern for the "veterans" in other children's theaters. I have seen girls go from age eight to age nineteen always being team players and taking the limited roles but never getting a lead role. It seemed to me that theater could be all about the artistic director, the "coach," and this served as another reminder that coaching basketball cannot be about the coach but must be about the girls. I realized that I had to make basketball better for the girls than what I had observed in the brutal field of performing arts.

On my girls' teams, including All Net, all the girls get fair playing time. One year at St. Mary's, my least talented girl got one basket in the course of the entire season. It was a putback under the basket at the end of the game, and we beat St. Martins by two points. They practically carried her off the floor. She was a star! I had another girl on an NJB team who had a similar non-offensive year but made a steal at the end of a game to preserve a one-point victory. *She* was the star for that moment.

In children's theater, the stars are chosen before the performance, before the curtain is raised. From year to year, they tend to be the same girls. At a fifth-grade girls' game at St. Mary's, when the first whistle is blown for the starting jump ball, any of ten girls can be the star. That is why I love grade school girls' basketball.

One of my pet peeves when it comes to priorities is the conflicts with other sports. In the Silicon Valley/Bay Area, it seems that basketball does not get the respect of sports such as volleyball and soccer. OK, I am a hoops-obsessed Hoosier, but why do the higher level club coaches for soccer and volleyball insist that their girls put basketball or any other sport as second priority, if they allow it at all? One year I tried that priority with my NJB All Net, the highest level of club basketball at that age, but all I accomplished was losing some of my top athletes who bowed to the soccer and volleyball gods. What is it with worshiping soccer in the Bay Area? Now, I believe Brandi Chastain is a living legend, and having met her and watched her play, I can only say she deserves all the adulation and more. But just as my girls are not going to be playing WNBA, we may have a long time to go before the Bay Area has another Brandi.

Dagney currently has a winter season conflict with club volleyball and school/club basketball.  The frustrating thing is that once Dagney is in high school there is no conflict; volleyball is in the fall and basketball is in the winter. Since both club teams are at the highest level, it looks like

Dagney may have to pick her sport at the age of twelve. Given the millions of dollars that parents pay to club sports sometimes I wonder what would happen if the same money were paid to the school athletic departments, the kids played for their school "club" teams, and the conflicts were managed by the schools.

I never saw a soccer game in my life until I moved to Los Gatos and Casey started playing club soccer. We were fortunate that despite my frustrations with soccer (which we will cover), Casey and then Sydney had excellent coaches who did not suffer from OCCD. In Los Gatos, recreational and/or club soccer starts at about age five. Our daughters began playing at age five with five on five, on a marked field a bit smaller than a basketball court and with no goalies. Every girl scored in the course of the season, and by the end of the season we were seeing scores of 13-11, 12-9, etc... . I was impressed that five-year-old girls were creating this much offense. The following year, seemingly as a response to the increased scoring, the league added goalies to the venue. At first, the goalies stopped everything and there was not much scoring. But as with the first year, the girls improved their skills, and by the end of the year we could have a 6-4 or 5-4 game.

The league's response to the scoring was to institute the offside rule the following year. The best I can understand, offside is a rule that ensures that offensive players cannot gain advantage on defensive players in this ongoing war against scoring. In later years, our daughters' coaches and opposing coaches supplemented the offside rule by putting their fastest girls on defense. Casey's club soccer team, under the excellent coaching of UK National team player Steve Wilson, was the exception; but it seems that by the time most teams reached "Under 15" level, scoring was nearly eliminated altogether. In fact, when we were lucky enough to get a 1-0 score, the goal was almost always a fluke, sometimes deflected off a swift defender's leg.

From what I can see, it only gets worse at the professional level. In a recent game in San Francisco, Barcelona and Chivas played a Saturday night exhibition game at Candlestick Park. More than sixty-one thousand fans watched ninety minutes of soccer that had a total of two scores, a 1-1 tie. Imagine this: If you allow one second per score, you have two seconds of scoring in a 5400-second game. Another way of looking at this soccer match is that there was scoring .03% of the game—and worse, there was no winner. Yet the headline in the following Sunday morning's *Mercury News* sports page read "It was quite a draw." There is so little scoring in soccer that a highly reputable sports section like that of the *San Jose Mercury News* was reduced to reporting on the *potential* of a score.

*In the eighth minute, Padilla found himself alone on the left side. He slipped past Barca's Carles Puyol with no one in front of him. But Padilla, who played for Monroe Middle High School, faced a difficult angle. He slammed the ball into the near post as the crowd let out a sigh in unison.*

*"You know what I would have done if I made that?" he said. "I would have gone crazy." So would have most of the 61,572 fans in attendance ...* blah, blah, blah.[2]

The World Cup is such a wonderful, emotional gathering of athletes from all corners of the world. Other than the Olympics there may not be a better international stage for bringing countries and cultures together. If only they allowed some scoring. And while they are at it, take the proceeds from one ticket sale and buy a transmitter for the referee's clock so that the actual time can be displayed for the paying fans to see.

The one thing that continues to puzzle me is the offside rule in soccer that limits scoring. Why create a rule to ensure low or no scoring in a game? Can you imagine if basketball had an offside rule? Imagine a timeout in basketball in which the coach is designing a strategy to turn around a one-point deficit with seconds to go.

"… and so, if the trap works and we intercept the pass, let's get to the middle. Kobe, you fill the first lane, but don't run too fast and get ahead of any defender. Make sure the defender is ahead of you so he has a fair chance to stop our fast break, we can't afford an offside call …"

I was actually beginning to enjoy soccer with Dagney, as she was extremely fast and was actually scoring some goals as a forward. Then we got a new coach who, in his zeal to support the 0-0 objective, put the fastest girls, including Dagney, on defense. She never scored again; nor did most her teammates. I did not complain when she chose to give up soccer and focus on other sports.

Volleyball was another sport I discovered in California. I like volleyball. They not only allow but actually encourage scoring. But I must admit that I will miss those beautiful sun filled, cool-breeze California autumn days on the soccer or field hockey sidelines. I enjoyed being with the soccer families, talking to the dads about that day's NCAA Big Ten and Pac Ten games, the possible bowl matchups, the upcoming NCAA hoops season and prospects, and . . oh yeah, watching the girls grind it out to an offside-laden 0-0 tie.

OK, I feel better now, after years of pent-up frustration watching my daughters' soccer games. I am sure that my good friends who love soccer will dismiss me as a misguided hick from Indiana. I must confess that they are probably right.

[1] San Jose Mercury News, January 23, 2009
[2] San Jose Mercury News, August 9, 2009, page C1

# 4

## PRACTICES

*"They say that nobody is perfect. Then they tell you practice makes perfect. I wish they'd make up their minds."*

–Wilt Chamberlain

Grade school basketball games at St. Mary's are comprised of four six-minute quarters. When you combine that with the school's proper policy of fair playing time, and you have ten or more girls on this non-cut sport ... well, you see that there is not a lot of actual playing time in an eight-game season. If you accept the earlier-mentioned priorities of improving girls' skills and enhancing their experience, then practice is the main venue for those objectives. You have to do your best to get everyone's focus for the precious practice time allotted. And you don't know what kind of day they may have had, or what seemingly trivial issue (to a coach) could be weighing heavily on their minds. The late and beloved coach Jim Valvano once asked a player, Chuck Nevitt, why he seemed nervous at a practice.

"My sister's expecting a baby, and I don't know if I'm going to be an uncle or an aunt," Nevitt allegedly said. And that was at the college level.

By far the biggest practice challenge at the fifth-grade girls level is keeping their attention. Girls at this age are coming into their own socially, and for many, basketball practice is another platform for social interaction. Like many coaches, I will stop instruction when I see side conversations, and make the girls "run the lines." This not only serves as a reminder to pay attention but also puts teammate pressure on the girl subject to verbal temptation.

At a kickoff practice with Dagney's school team, the girls were super hyper; after *three* interruptions to run the lines in a five-minute span, I noticed Brynn, a talented but highly social athlete, take her place alone along the wall, gasping for air. Her nine teammates sat along the center-line as I revisited offensive alignments. "Brynn," I asked, "Why are you not joining your teammates?"

"Coach, *gasp*, I just can't control my talking, *gasp*, and I don't think I can, *gasp*, survive another line run." I was impressed with her self-disciplinary action, but it reminded me of my competition for the mind share of ten-year-old girls.

I always plan ahead and schedule our time (1-1.5 hours) with activities in increments of ten minutes. I start with stretching (never too young for proper stretching, especially in cold gyms) and a few laps around the gym.

I always schedule ten minutes of oratory, where I might discuss the last game or talk about the plan for the next game. These sessions many times fail to meet the objective; ten-year-old girls love to participate, many times trying to better the oral presentation of the girl who went before her. I always seem to shut these sessions off minutes beyond my scheduled time and halfway through my agenda. I begin the verbal session by having them sit on the gym floor, facing me as I stand against the wall beyond the basket, as it takes very little to distract them. If they are facing another team practicing on the other half court, there is no hope for their attention beyond my first sentence.

One activity I like to do when reviewing a past game is to ask each girl to list the best thing she did in the game and the best thing a teammate did. This is an exercise in building both their self-esteem and the teamwork ethic.

You learn a lot about a ten-year-old girl in these exchanges —and it can be so hard sometimes to keep a straight face. Alisa, on Dagney's fifth-grade St. Mary's team, stated that her best contribution in the win over St. Lucy's was "my assist to Brynn under the basket." When I asked her about the best thing a teammate did in the game she replied, "Brynn making the basket so I could get the assist." Smart girl.

Sometimes they say things that break a coach's heart. A girl on one of my St. Mary's teams, while a very smart student, was short, a true hoops beginner, and the most timid of all the girls. When I asked her about a teammate's contribution, she asked me, "Can it be more than one teammate?"

"Of course," I answered, encouraged that I was actually getting her involved in the exercise.

"The best thing my teammates did was when the girls on the bench yelled out the seconds on the clock when I had the ball at the end of the third quarter."

"That's great. And what was *your* biggest contribution?"

"I did not have one. It was like when I heard them get to two seconds, I shot the ball and it went under the backboard."

"Honey, you just made a great contribution, explaining how even girls on the bench can contribute to the team." Seeing a smile break out on her humble face made me just as happy. That dialogue reminded me of Moses Malone, a great NBA center who gave credit for his leading rebounding to his teammates, for missing most of their shots.

I sometimes use the dialogue session for a motivational speech. I always remember my high school coach's speeches and I have aspired to motivate my girls the way he motivated me.

One Saturday morning I decided to make a special motivational speech for my fifth-grade girls prior to the All Net Post-Season Tournament. This was a team with a history of winning, but we faced some strong upcoming competition in the tournament and I felt I needed to get them motivated to new heights. I wore the green Larry Bird Boston Celtics shirt that Casey had gotten me for Christmas. Coach Pat and I gathered the ten girls in a semi-circle around the free throw lane, away from any distractions in the now-silent gymnasium, and I began my "sermon on the line."

"Larry Bird and I played in the same high school conference in southern Indiana. (Suddenly I realized only my daughter Dagney knew who Larry Bird was, but I forged on.) I could dunk and I was fast. He could barely dunk with one hand, could not jump and was slow. He went on to be the greatest player in the NBA and I went on to be a robot salesman. Why, you would ask? (Nobody was asking yet.) Larry went on to be one of the *greatest* professional basketball players *ever* because Larry worked harder than me and practiced more than I did; he worked on weaknesses, like his left hand, while I worked on my strengths, like baseline jumpers. (I left out the detail of Larry being a superior athlete, for effect.) Larry once spent an entire summer as a thirty-year-old Celtic working on his left-handed shots around the basket, alone in his humid Springs Valley high school gym. Larry gave 100% on the floor every game, whether offense or defense, just like our Sophie. Sophie is last running lines in practice, yet she is the first girl to the other end in transition during the game. *That* is the kind of hustle Larry Bird brought to the game of basketball. This is the kind of hustle *all* of you girls can bring to the game tomorrow. Tomorrow we need to look within ourselves and find our Sophie, our Larry Bird, our … " I eloquently waxed on, raising the tempo just like my old coaches, and I was getting close to the crescendo, the big climax, feeling goose bumps on my arms when suddenly Dagney raised her hand. I'm thinking she is finally going to show leadership and deliver the big close, as she and her sisters had suffered through my soliloquies of adulation for Bird many times.

"Yes, Dagney?" I said, thinking, *"Bring it on, my baby daughter!"*

"I just lost my tooth." She held it up with a big toothless smile while nine other girls clamored around her, oohing and aahing … After each girl fondled the tooth, we did lay-ups with outlet passes, my attempt at an inspirational speech a distant memory. It was one of my many failures in attempting to fire up my teams with a motivational speech. I came to envy the electricity and excitement generated from the team mom handing out stylish warm-up sweaters and pants.

I also use the practice talking sessions for some Basketball 101 and basketball vocabulary lessons, which will be addressed in a later chapter. The Basketball 101 stuff involves describing game situations and asking the girls what they should do. Such as: What should a team do who has the ball with thirty seconds left and a four-point lead? Or: What should the other team on defense do in the same situation? At this age, the girls want so very badly to be able to provide the right answer that it forces not only deep thought but also, in the end, the correct answer is remembered.

Recently Pat, my good friend and our assistant All Net coach, asked our fifth-grade girls the question, "When is the only time on defense that you should not box out on a shot?" I watched all ten girls frowning, grimacing, wanting *so* badly to be able to provide the right answer. Alena, perhaps our best defender, raised her hand and then quickly took it down, along with her eyes. DB, one of the brightest girls and a tenacious defender, did the same. I was struggling with the question myself, so I was surprised when Dagney raised her hand with a look of 100% confidence.

"When you are sitting on the bench." On the drive home that night, Dagney challenged why that was not an accurate answer, that I always said the girls on the bench are part of the game. I had to concede that technically she was right.

I think most youth basketball coaches begin practices with lay-ups; one line makes the lay-up while the other line gets the rebound and passes to the "passing girl" in the corner. The "passing girl" makes a lead pass to the next girl in the lay-up line. The use of the "passing girl" is a good tool to teach the girls not to pass to the girl but to where you want the girl to be. You switch lay-up shooting sides to ensure the weak hand gets equal or more time. I believe coaches need to teach by example, so I line up with the girls for the lay-ups. I emphasize that the shooting hand rises toward the backboard in tandem with the same side knee, as if there were a puppet string connecting the shooting wrist to the knee. I verbalize this as I shoot from both sides. After my instructions at one of Casey's fifth-grade practices, where each of my lay-ups fell perfectly into the rim, I got a question from teammate Kelly. Up to that night, Kelly had been coming off the bench as a reserve forward.

"Coach, how many years did you star at Purdue?" Kelly started in the next game against Queen of Apostles.

That same year, we followed the fifth-grade boys' practice. One night, after we warmed up with lay-ups and I did the instructional verbalizing as I laid in my bank shots, I got a question from Rusty, a classmate of Casey's who was watching from the sideline.

"Excuse me, Mr. Duncheon; did you play in the NBA?" On the drive home that night I told Casey she should someday marry a nice boy like Rusty.

"Dad, can't you see he is such a suck-up?" she replied, and did the gag simulation with her index finger in her mouth, rolling down her car window for effect. I did not fall for the act; I had it on good authority (Caitlin #1) that she had a crush on Rusty.

These car rides from practice proved to be a key part of the bond with my daughters that basketball provided me. No television or computer in front of their faces, we could only talk; it was the venue in which I found out why Casey liked the Backstreet Boys, that Good Charlotte was Sydney's favorite band and not a good friend, and that Hannah Montana and Miley Cyrus were one and the same.

And the bartering of flattery for playing time carried through all the way to Dagney's St. Mary's team. While getting organized at practice for the St. Mary's opener against St. Lucy's, Ashley (who is most fashionable in her own right) remarked, "Coach, that is such a smart sweater/shirt combination you have on today," prompting my offhanded yet misguided response, "Why thank you, Ashley. That kind of compliment can get you more playing time against Lucy's."

This led to nonstop flattery throughout the practice: "Nice haircut, Coach....Are those new shoes?....Coach, you are really stylin'....Now I know where Dagney gets her good taste in clothes.....etc, etc. etc." We only won by one point against Lucy's, but I thought twice about what I wore to the game. I never stop learning about the impact one statement can make on these girls' hyperactive minds.

So back then and still today, after stretches, a couple of laps, lay-ups and some dialogue, we do some of the fundamental X's and O's. Then we usually move to some floor fundamentals and drills. In early season practices, especially for school teams with little hoops experience, much of the practice is drills. I drill everything from passing to lay-ups to moving feet on defense. I try to teach peripheral vision, having a girl facing the basket at the top of the key identify how many fingers I hold up in one wing position and how many another teammate is hold up in the other wing position, while looking directly between us at the rim of the basket. This teaches the girls how to watch the girl with the ball and the girl she is defending at the same time. During the eighth-grade year on Casey's team, I had to create a rule that a single finger could be only the index finger, after an incident using the middle finger led to ball hurling and teenage drama.

There are endless challenges in teaching fundamentals when you have two or three hours to practice a week. I stress the need to practice at home in the driveway, and to pick a day to do all things, including opening doors and writing, with your weak hand. Many of the challenges evolve around dribbling the ball. I have always preached the doctrine that dribbling is one of basketball's necessary evils: that a passed ball moves faster than a dribbled ball, dribbling should be done *toward* the basket and not sideways or away from the hoop, and if you can't dribble toward the basket you should only dribble to protect the ball from the a defender. Some of my biggest fundamental challenges for young girls have always been:

1. Dribbling only when you have to; passing is the first option.
2. Dribbling the ball while looking ahead at the players on the court.
3. Dribbling with the hand opposite the defender, even if it is the weak hand.
4. Not picking up the dribble until you know you are going to pass or shoot.

5.  Not standing still, but spreading out or moving to an open area to receive a pass.
6.  Boxing out the opposition while rebounding.
7.  Moving feet first on defense, not hands.
8.  Moving the foot first on the drive, then the dribble.
9.  Avoiding taking the ball to the "graveyard" (the lower baseline corners).

One challenge I have always had with young girls is to get them to be physical. At one practice with one of my more passive 5th grade teams I reminded the girls that basketball was not just a contact sport, but a collision sport. I told them if they did not like physical bumps with girls they don't know that they should play badminton. I asked how many wanted to play badminton instead of basketball; no hands were raised. Then we did a drill where I used a floor mat to bump the girls as they attempted their layups. I was trying to get them focused on making the layup even with strong physical contact from the defender and getting that chance for the three point play. After a few bumps some girls were actually making the layup with big smiles despite the mat bump. But then ten minutes later during my boxing out drill one girl knocked her teammate to the floor, apologized profusely, and then avoided any physical contact the rest of the night. It's hard to get ten year old girls comfortable with proactively making physical contact with others on the floor. But when you have one who does like it, you have a potential Division I athlete.

After fifteen years of grade school coaching, I admit I may never get ten year old kids to box out, at least the non-NJB club girls. I am proud to say I have gotten my girls to dribble down the court without looking at the ball. I accomplished that with a method gained from my fifth-grade experience at St. Peter's in Montgomery, Indiana. Our coach started with shop safety glasses, then stuck tape across the lower halves of the lenses. First we lined up with bent knees and dribbled with the strong hand, then the left hand, all the while not being able to see the ball. Then we crossed hand to hand. Once we had a level of confidence in the stationary mode, he had us dribble to lines of chairs on the floor, crossing over to the opposite hand at each chair.

The chair drill always became interesting with the girls. I would line up two opposing teams in a relay with two rows of chairs. Balls were kicked, balls clanged into chairs, girls kicked chairs over, chairs would fly into the other row, sometimes followed by girls doing the same ... frankly, I am lucky no one was injured. But I saw progress by mid-season, and fifth-grade girls who can dribble up the court without looking at the ball can make fast break passes for lay-ups. Well, make that attempted lay-ups. The lay-up is another fundamental that must be squeezed into those two hours per week.

Another good drill for teaching the girls to keep their eyes off the dribble is the "last dribbler" drill. During this drill, all the girls dribble their ball within the baseline and three-point arc line. The objective is to knock another girl's ball out of the area while maintaining her own dribble. Hands are switched at the blow of the whistle. I have had lots of smiles and laughs with this drill.

Moving away from the ball on offense is another tough fundamental for young girls to learn. I tried to teach a mindset to always be in a position where a defender can't reach out and tag you. I invented some "tag" games in drills that helped build this mindset while having fun.

A drill that teaches movement away from the ball—and also works on that daunting instinct for ten-year-olds to dribble all the time—is to play a game at one end of the court in which you can't dribble, you can only pass.

If young basketball girls are competitive at all, they will love basketball obstacle course competition. One of my drills starts with the girl diving under an outstretched floor mop for a loose ball, picking it up and dribbling toward a chair in the middle of the court, crossing over to the other hand and dribbling to the basket for a lay-up, dribbling back with the other hand toward the chair, crossing over to the other hand and then making a lay-up, all timed with the stopwatch. It gets even more interesting with the taped shop glasses. To keep the team concept, I some-times do this drill in relay form with five on each team.

Improving shooting skills at the fifth-grade level is so important, especially when you consider you will face the packed-in 2-1-2 zone defenses that only allow longer shots. A drill that teaches *game pressure* shooting skills as well as rebounding and that is popular with my girls is a competition shoot-and-rebound drill. Each team has two players. For a one or two-minute cycle, one girl is a shooter while the other rebounds and passes. Then they switch roles for the next time cycle. The shooter takes five designated shots along the outside of the paint, then three shots at designated spots outside the three-point line. Each score along the paint is one point for the team and each three-pointer is two points. Any missed shot that is rebounded by the non-shooting teammate without the ball hitting the ground gets one point for the team. The shooter keeps shooting the cycle until the time is up. Multiple goals allow simultaneous cycles. The girls love the contest; they end up huffing and puffing, and it teaches good teamwork.

Another of the challenges I have had with young girls is that of motivation, especially at practices. Different levels of basketball require different motivational strategies. At the AAU or NJB All Net level, most girls are there because they love hoops. You can motivate them by challenging them to improve in overall hoops skills. I like to motivate all levels of girls by complimenting them on specific achievements in front of the whole team during the X's and O's sessions. On the other hand, it is important to communicate one-on-one to each "non-starter" about what it takes for her to be a starter, or for any girl to get more playing time. I had one All Net fifth grader ask why she did not play more, given that she was a good outside shooter. I told her she needed to improve her defense, moving her feet and rotating to help her fellow teammates on defense. I told her that if for every basket she scored she gave up one at the other end, the net contribution was zero. The worst way to treat a fifth grader is to bench her for non-performance and not specifically communicate the non-performance and how it can be overcome. A good player can sit on the bench confused, disillusioned and unmotivated without clear, instructive communication.

Girls at the lower levels, typically recreational league and most school teams, require different strategies for motivation. Making practice fun and mixing in non-basketball mental games can motivate them to want to come back to practice again. It is important to create drills that a lesser skilled player can win. "Land! Sea! Air!"-type line jumping games that require quick thinking with footwork are not basketball drills, but are enjoyed by young girls and allow some girls to win who are unlikely to win at a basketball drill contest. In this drill the girls line up on one side of the three point line, on "land". If the coach calls out "sea", they jump across the line to the "sea". If he calls out "land" they have to stay feet in place. If he calls out "air" they have to jump up but stay in their "land" or "sea" side of the line. Calling the commands at a quick place creates fun competition for the girls and enhances reflexes, independent of basketball skills.

One method I have found very effective, especially for fourth- and fifth-grade girls, is to motivate with candy. I kept a full bag of chocolate and other unhealthy treats in the ball bag. Candy would become the reward for everything, from the girl who came in first running the lines to the girl who won the jumping contest, to the "Land! Sea! Air!" contest, to the last remaining dribbler in the dribble-in-the-paint contest … and I end each practice with the girls making one three-point attempt, any winner gets candy. After the three-point-shooting exercise, I allow the winning girls from all contests to take their pick from the goody bag. This practice was not always popular with the parents; I did receive occasional complaints about sugar highs at bedtime and had one parent promise (in jest, I hope) to send me the dental bills. Dana once told me I was reduced to treating Dagney the same way I motivated our dog, Louie the Loser, nicknamed for his bad hygiene habits, which I tried to change with dog treats. But I stand by this methodology as, unlike Louie, who did not cure his bad hygiene, the candy has motivated girls to improve their skills while also providing self-esteem.

If you are a father coaching your daughter's team, I highly recommend getting a female assistant coach or trainer. I have been lucky in recent years in having Sydney's good friend Kate, whom I coached in her grade school years, assist our assistant coach and me. The girls loved her, and frankly, she got through to them on many topics better than two male coaches could.

Of course, basketball employs both physical and mental skills. One of the mental concentration drills is to train the girls to focus on the shot and not be distracted by the defender. To teach that skill and to have fun, I set up a drill in which one row of girls lines up under the basket as defenders and another row of girls stands to the right of the basket as a shooter. I pass the ball to the next shooter and the next defender does two things:

1. Jump up and down with her arms waving.
2. Shout anything that comes to mind to distract the shooter.

This drill was successful the first time I used it with Casey's fifth-grade team. The girls learned that no matter how much motion the defender made and how much noise emitted from her mouth, the shot could be made by concentrating. By the time Casey reached eighth grade, the shouted distractions were getting a little out of hand. The progression of insults over time went something like this:

"Hey shooter!"

"Hey, miss it!"

"Hey ball!"

"You're a bad shooter!"

"You like Rusty!"

"Rusty hates you!"

"Bugger in your nose!"

"Nice zit!"

"Tiny boobs!"

The tiny boobs insult led to the only time I saw three voluntary laps around the gym, as the insulter ran for her life from the shooter, who gave up on the shot and bounced the ball off the insulter's head. Just short of a brawl, I decided to stop the distraction/focus drills after sixth grade.

There are many other drills I have used, but the best summary I can provide is to focus on drills that teach vital hoops skills while creating fun. Also, it is important for all the girls to be involved at all times. Since practice time is so precious, it makes no sense for two girls to be doing a drill while eight watch, many times chatting among themselves. One way to help that objective within tight budgets is to have each girl bring her own ball, if she owns one. Then all ten girls can be involved at the same time in dribbling and shooting drills. Last, I would recommend making sure there are drills that each girl can win.

After fundamentals, we work on offensive and defensive "alignments." I say alignments, as I usually stay away from set plays. I learned that at this age, if you call a play, the girls will execute the exact series of events, even if it means passing the ball directly to a defender. Instead, I try to get the girls to align in one way against a zone, another against a man-to-man and another for out of bounds under the basket, and to get the other four girls to move away from the ball. This makes the offense more opportunistic and teaches the girls hoops instincts, to look for and see scoring opportunities that require at least two players to create.

After offensive and defensive alignments, we finish with scrimmaging. When parents show up to pick up their kids, they are able to watch them in what is close to a real game. I don't mind parents at practices. My only rule with parents at practices and games is that they not provide direction for their girls, just cheers and support. There can be only one voice providing guidance on the floor and that must come from the coaches' bench. I found that this rule, plus playing time policies and basketball priorities vs. other sports or events are best communicated in an email at the start of the season, to all parents.

Another tool I have found to be effective for young female basketball players is the Hoops Skills Assessment Sheet. In essence, I list all hoops skills ranging from passing to rebounding to lay-ups to defensive footwork. What I discovered is that if you fill out a form for each girl early in the season and have a one-on-one session with them, they really work to improve the specific skills you ask them to improve. I always try to balance the "needs improvement" parts with the "good for fifth grade" or "better than most fifth graders" on each girl's assessment. Dagney and most fifth graders take their report cards seriously, and they see this assessment sheet as a basketball report card. At the end-of-season party, I emphasize skill improvement for each girl. Feedback is *so* motivational at this age, especially positive feedback.

A drill I do at the end of All Net practices is "last girl to hit a free throw"—the contest that no girl wants to win. Five girls rotate at both ends, shooting one free throw at a time. No girl can leave the gym until she hits a free throw and no one wants to be the last one to make it. It is a good pressure free-throw shooting drill and I only use it at the highest level, the All Net team. If I used it at St. Mary's it would not be good for some of the girls' self-esteem, not to mention we might be there all night.

There are differences in the series of activities in fifth-grade girls' NJB club basketball practices and the school practices, mostly the level of intensity. But one thing I always try to do, especially at the school level, is to find a way for the weakest athlete to make a contribution during the scrimmage, and hopefully later in a game. It is almost worth keeping a notebook on the bench during games, as it is so easy to forget those small contributions that can make such a positive impact on a young girl if you mention it in front of her peers. I loved the smile from a less-skilled fifth-grade girl at the end of one scrimmage when I told her, "Great rebound, you out-jumped the other nine girls for that one!"

Remember the Dave Najour adage, "This will be the last time they play organized basketball ... " Make it a wonderful memory.

# 5

## 10-Year-Old Female Vocabulary

*"I told him, 'Son, what is it with you? Is it ignorance or apathy?' He said, 'Coach, I don't know and I don't care.'"*

–Frank Layden, Utah Jazz president, on a former player

By now I have almost mastered communication with 10-year-old girls, just in time for my impending retirement from coaching! Early on with Casey's teams, I discovered that ten-year-old girls are very literal. And why not? They have only been speaking this language for eight years or so.

I remember one night at fifth-grade practice trying to get Brittnay to be more aggressive in receiving passes, corralling rebounds, and scooping up loose balls.

"Brittnay, that's YOUR ball! Brittnay, you gotta want it, it's YOUR ball! C'mon Brittnay, dive for it, it's YOUR ball!" I repeated.

At a water break, Brittnay came to me with a serious look in her deep brown eyes, asking, "Coach, why do you keep saying it's my ball? Don't you recognize your own daughter's ball? It has Casey's name on it." She turned her back, drinking from her water bottle and shaking her head, thinking her coach was losing his mind.

I was frustrated at one of my fifth-grade team's practices about the lack of communication among teammates on the court. There was no calling out "pick!" The girl taking it from under the basket might meekly mutter "break," or I might hear a muted "switch" on a pick, if anything was said at all. I was particularly frustrated when a girl dribbling down the court on a fast break had a defender come from behind and knock the ball away three different times, while her four teammates yelled no warning for her.

"Girls," I said, "You got to *scream* out a warning when your teammate is about to get caught from behind! Next time that happens I want to hear you scream." Of course "Behind you!", "Crossover!" or "Watch out behind!" all would have sufficed, but as Dagney was dribbling with another defender close behind her, Dagney's teammate suddenly stopped in her tracks, rolled her head back, spread her arms outward dramatically and screamed, yes *screamed* at the top of her lungs,

"EEEEEEEEEEEEEEEEEH!," just as I had asked.

In an inner team scrimmage with the fourth-grade recreational league girls, I was attempting to get my girls to understand the difference between the first shot of a two-shot foul being dead and the second shot being live for rebounds. Roslyn had gone about 0 for 12 already from the field and had been fouled by Sydney. I lined up all the girls on the free throw line. Just prior to handing the ball to Roslyn for her first shot, I said, "OK, girls, this shot is dead."

An embarrassed Roslyn cried out in agony, "Coach, how can you say it's a missed shot before I even shoot? You hurted my feelings!"

"I'm sorry, Roslyn, that is not what I meant. Girls, after Roslyn shoots the ball at the basket, and if it does not go in and if you have a chance to get the rebound, you can get it but you have to give it to me, because it is only the first of two shots that Roslyn has been awarded, and if it goes in she also gets a second shot ... " *God, what was I doing?*

Sydney looked at her teammates and said, "Girls, stay put on Roslyn's first shot." Roslyn missed her thirteenth shot and nobody moved.

In a third- and fourth-grade NJB game, we were trailing by two points with thirty seconds to go and the West San Jose team had the ball. I had no timeouts left so I yelled from the bench, "Foul the girl with the ball, we have to foul the girl with the ball!" West San Jose's best ball handler kept dribbling and I noticed that my Missy guarding her did *not* foul her but stayed with her, even on the wrong side of the dribbler. She remained one step behind the dribbler, and without touching her, followed her into the paint and to the basket, where the dribbler made the game-clinching lay-up. I asked Missy after the game why she was not fouling the girl. She replied, "Oh, I thought you said I should be *following* her."

After several communication sessions, I came to better understand the state of ten-year-old girls' minds and perceptions. I realized that girls immediately assign meaning to the spoken word as they hear it. Thinking back to my own grade school days also helped me understand that. Until the fifth grade I understood the mascot of St. Peters to be the "Blue Goats." When I got my first blue and gold uniform as a fifth-grade player and experienced the first cheer-block cheer, it suddenly dawned on me that we were actually the "Blue Golds." Kids can only read so much; the rest of their mental growth comes through what they hear.

I also discovered that in this California world where basketball is just one of many activities for kids the parents can take spoken words from the bench literally as well. In a St. Mary's game against St. Andrews we scored a basket to get us within three with ninety seconds to go. I had no timeouts left and could only yell instructions from the bench as I tried to get the girls to put on a man to man full court press. "Get a girl!" I yelled. "Tie her up!" I added to Ashley whose girl received an inbound pass in the corner. Dana told me later that it was about that time that Ashley's mother, Denise turned to her with a stunned look on her face.

"Get a girl, tie her up!?!" questioned Denise. "Should we be saying that at a Catholic school?"

From the beginning of my coaching career, I have added some academics to each practice. In covering activity in the classroom prior to practice, I heard terms like the "Specific Ocean," "Taking things for granite," "Placing the reef at the tomb of the Unknown Soldier," and many others. I laughed at Sydney's remark that one of her St. Mary's classmates did not do well on her religion test. Trying to write the Lord's Prayer, she opened with "Our Father who *aren't* in heaven" and ended with "lead us not into temptation but deliver us *some email,* Amen." After a couple years, I decided to institute another activity in the early academic dialogue session of practices: the basketball vocabulary lesson.

My theme here was that smart basketball players had an edge and that academics were still the top priority of student athletes. I would remind the girls that curse words are used by those who can't make their points because of their weak vocabularies. At each practice, I would choose a word and challenge the girls to:

1. Provide the definition
2. Use it in a basketball sentence.

I chose words that were challenging and also applied to the game of hoops. Most of these exercises resulted in good vocabulary lessons. An example: I introduced *transition* and involved two of the smartest girls I coached. Ally immediately provided the definition, "To go through a change, coach?"

"Excellent, Ally! Now who can use it in a sentence?"

Isabel looked to the sky for a moment and then raised her hand. "If we miss the basket and they get the rebound, we need to make a transition to guard them."

"Outstanding, girls!" It was great to see the girls increasing their vocabulary and learning the game at the same time. But it did not always go that perfectly.

You will recall the peripheral vision drill with the fingers. Peripheral vision is so important in hoops that I also tried to get a mental mindset around it. One of the first words I used in my lesson was *peripheral*, obviously looking for the use of peripheral vision on the court. After lay-ups at one practice, I gathered Casey's fifth-grade girls together for the vocabulary word. I got the proper definition immediately from Genna. Then Janelle volunteered the basketball sentence. "After I accidentally kicked the ball out of bounds and went over to pick it up I saw Caitlin #1 laughing at me with my peripheral vision." Janelle was not utilizing her peripheral vision, as her deep blue eyes glared directly at Caitlin #1.

One of the words I used for all my teams was *tenacious*, looking for the adjective to be used in a sentence about defense. My girls in this case were stumped by the word. Lauren asked if it was a vegetable. I then gave my Webster's definition, "Tenacious: .....tending to adhere to another substance. Now can anybody use it in a basketball sentence?" Each time I've conducted these sessions, all of the girls want so badly to have the right definition or to use it properly in a basketball sentence, and this time was no exception. All eight girls were grimacing, frowning, wanting to raise their hands. Then suddenly dark brown-eyed Becky repeatedly pumped her hand in the air chanting, "Oo! Oo! Oo!"

"Becky, in a basketball sentence, please," I acknowledged.

Becky, first glancing at the other seven girls to make sure she had everyone's attention, responded, "My sister did like a tenacious dance with a St. Lucy's boy at the St. Martin's dance Friday night and got into trouble." There was silence as I thought about my response, uncomfortable with the territory she had introduced.

"Becky, that was not a basketball sentence."

She quickly responded, "Oh, and it was on the St. Martin's basketball floor," looking around at her teammates with the pride of being privy to this "scandal."

At one fourth-grade recreational league practice, I was trying to get the focus on moving feet and not reaching arms on defense. I decided that *appendage* was the word, and I would get some sentences on moving the proper appendages. Alexis got close on the definition: "A part of the body that sticks out."

Then I got a quick hand from auburn haired and freckled Kerry, "I can use it in a basketball sentence, Coach!"

"OK, Kerry, go ahead."

"The mean girl on the Pacers was like elbowing my tummy so hard I thought I was going to have to have my appendage removed."

Over time, I worked with the girls to break the word into its syllables and roots to determine the meaning. One practice, before playing a very good Holy Spirit team, I chose *fortitude*. Point guard Kate enthusiastically raised her hand with confidence, but power forward Katheryn had already begun her syllable breakdown as she stared at the ceiling.

"*Fort*... a place for the army to be safe; *-itude*, like gratitude ... being thankful to be safe in the fort ... being in a safe place." She was going nowhere near a basketball definition when Helena interrupted,

"Coach, that's not the meaning but I can use it in a sentence. At the end of the first quarter the score was four to tude." She was beaming with pride and Kate was shaking her head.

At an NJB practice I wanted to get my two point guards focused on distributing the ball, so the word I chose was *distribute*. I was pleased by an immediate volunteer from one of the point guards, Danielle, who was smart and also a talented softball pitcher. "To do something nice for a teammate."

"Well, maybe, but could you use it in a basketball sentence, Danielle?" Danielle went into thinking mode, drawing her brown eyes upward toward the gym ceiling with her fist clenched under her chin. Then she came up with the sentence, actually a paragraph.

"I did a distribute to Tessa at a basketball practice. She got mad at me because she said I was dissing her. But I explained that a distribute sounds like a dis but it is actually a tribute. That's why they call it a distribute." I was impressed with Danielle's innovative thinking.

Recently, at our first All Net practice, I wanted to emphasize the need to play a "smothering" man-to-man defense, given our lack of size. I introduced *asphyxiate*. But when I heard Emily breaking out the syllables, "ass – fix – I – ate," I disrupted the process, immediately provided the definition and allowed her to use it properly in a basketball sentence.

At a fifth-grade All Net club practice I was trying to get the girls to focus on the transition from defense to offense. I chose *fluidic* as the word, with hopes of the girls thinking of moving down the fast break in a fluidic motion, as in one common stream. I got off to a rare good start, and even rarer that it was with my missing-toothed Dagney. "A … fluid, like water, like moving on the court like water."

"Excellent, Dagney! Now who can use it in a basketball sentence?"

My three-point shooter Delaney immediately raised her hand and responded with her nose scrunched upward, "Even though Coach told me to put a body on number 23 Sunday, I couldn't do it 'cause she was like all sweaty and fluidic and gross!"

*Most* of the time I believe the girls learned the proper word definitions and subsequently used them to improve their vocabulary. On Casey's school team we had that model teammate, Genna. Genna was a very good point guard, a straight A student who always provided positive support for her teammates, both on the floor and on the bench. Two games after a lesson on the word *ambidextrous*, Genna yelled out to the floor after Casey made a left-handed lay-up, "Casey, you are SO amphibious!" But Genna was in good company, as Charles Shackleford, who played at North Carolina State and the NBA, was reported to use the same *amphibious* term describing his equal abilities in both hands.

At a sixth-grade practices with Sydney's team, Lauren, concerned she was not getting enough shots, offered to use *precision* twice in one basketball sentence, a first and only occurrence in my experience with these vocabulary lessons. "Sydney could have made a precision pass to me when I was open under the basket, but she took a un-precision shot instead." I told Lauren that would be "an" un-precision shot and to take up the passing issue one-on-one with Sydney.

At another practice I wanted to stress the need to develop all aspects of the game beyond shooting: passing, rebounding, defense, being able to play guard or forward … so I introduced *versatile*. Once again I got no takers on the definition, so I provided, "Embracing a variety of subjects, fields or skills; turning with ease from one thing to another … Who can use it in a basketball sentence?"

Madison was all over it with her right hand thrusting into the air. "Yes, Madison."

"Katherine was like very versatile with all the different pizzas at the school picnic and that's why she threw up at basketball practice."

My all-time favorite vocabulary lesson came when I was coaching a St. Mary's fifth-grade boys' team. These were a smart group of guys, so I tried to stump them with *ubiquitous*. Adam, Andrew, Austin, Will, and John had been getting the words all year but were struggling with this one. Indeed, no one could give me a definition, and then Chris raised his hand and offered, "Coach I can't give the exact definition but I can use it in a sentence."

"Go ahead."

"Coach, when we are at practice and we are goofing around and not hustling, you-bitch-at-us."

# 6

## TIMEOUTS: THE 60-SECOND CRITICAL MESSAGE

*"If you meet the Buddha in the lane, feed him the ball."*
–Phil Jackson, Lakers coach

Sometime in the 1990s, at least for me, the term "elevator pitch" became a common phrase in the venture capital lexicon of the Silicon Valley. The "elevator pitch" term represented how you would communicate your company's value in the most positive way to a venture capitalist, if you only had the time of an elevator ride together. In other words, what can you say about your company in sixty seconds that would make an investor want to invest in it? I have to say that in 1999 I successfully made such pitches twice that led to investors in a company I started. But I also have to confess that I was not as successful in sixty-second pitches at fifth grade and third grade girls' timeouts that same year. We have covered the challenges of communicating to ten-year-olds at basketball practices; it only becomes more challenging in a timeout when you have the sixty-second constraint.

One thing I have come to appreciate in coaching is the precious commodity called the timeout. Depending on the league, you may get only four per game, sixty seconds each. Sometimes they throw in a couple thirty-second allocations. Grade school and young club team coaches do not get the advantage of the college and pro coaches, who are accommodating the TV commercials and are afforded well past sixty seconds. If you notice, the head coaches first take time to converse with their assistant coaches while the players get water and take their seats, then they discuss strategy for multiple minutes. Not so with us young girl coaches; we have sixty seconds. I have learned first to be conservative with the use of timeouts early in games, saving as many as possible for the end of the game.

I have also learned to make sure I am prepared to effi-
ciently communicate a vital game-saving message in those
precious thirty or sixty seconds. One of the biggest challenges I have ever experienced is calling my last timeout
when the game is close, and needing to convey a critical
change in game strategy in seconds to ten-year-old female
minds.

Time for my next confession … my many failures in
certain communications with the fairer sex under pressure
situations. You might think that growing up as the only
male in a four-person family would have made me sensitive to female feelings, thus making communication easier.
But the truth is that much of the communication with my
sisters and mother made no sense to me. Rather than try
to understand what made them tick, I would pull away,
put the transistor radio plug in my ear and listen to Jack
Buck and Harry Carey announce a St. Louis Cardinals
baseball game.

I think most guys have gone through those pressure situations with their other halves. Such as, what do you say
when you come home from a pickup hoops game and
beers with your buddies and realize you missed an anniversary … the date you met, the first date, etc.? This is
good practice for coaching in timeout situations. You have
a specific amount of time, first to respond to the situation
the game has handed you, and then to communicate successfully. If you take too much time for the initial
response, you lose, you are cooked ("I was going to surprise you later tonight") and anything else you say has no
credibility. On the other hand, if you take a few seconds,

gather your excuse in your head and then deliver the message, it has to be perfect or you lose again, e.g., saying you
flew back over the international date line and got your
days confused. I have spent many corporate years in sales
situations and communicated fairly successfully. Elevator
pitches aside, the difference between selling million dollar
projects in a corporate situation and a timeout is that in
selling you have more than ten or sixty seconds to respond
to tough questions and if you are a good salesman, you
have prepared yourself for any question. This does not
apply to a forgotten anniversary or a sudden sixty-second
timeout to stop an eight-point run by the opposing team.

I will share a example of a one of my attempts to communicate with women effectively in a time-pressured situation. A couple of years out of college, on a hot, humid
night in Creve Coeur, Missouri, I was in the laundromat
under the clubhouse of my apartment complex. I had
come to pick up my clothes from the dryer after my hoops
game and was drenched in sweat. Discovering my jeans
were still wet and I had no additional quarters for the
dryers, I chose to stuff them into the dryer of an attractive
young woman who had left, presumably for the cooler
confines of her apartment. I assumed it was a safe move,
figuring I only needed a few minutes, until she suddenly
reappeared with her novel and sat down across from her
dryer of "whites" rotating with my jeans. The first pressured communication came when I confessed that I had
stuffed my jeans into her whites. Following her immediate
instructions, I opened the dryer door to remove the jeans,
but the door sensor was not working and the dryer kept

rotating. Fighting back the hurling whites with my arms and chest, I finally withdrew my jeans and slammed the door shut. When I approached her again to apologize, I discovered one of her "unmentionables" clinging to my sweaty shoulder. The second pressured communication was upon me. I handed her the garment and all I could muster was, "You might want to wash this again." I promptly tossed the jeans in my basket and departed, never looking back.

Years later, I found myself in another pressure situation asking for immediate communication. Over the years basketball took its toll on my knees, and I had decided to mix in some other less joint-demanding exercises. I chose to participate in an early morning stationary bike spinning class at a Los Gatos health club. The class was mostly women; I usually took a bike in the back row so I would not be noticed if I did not keep up with the rest of the class. After a few sessions, I found myself keeping up and feeling the benefits, in response to a most demanding (and very fit) woman instructor. This woman had no body fat, never smiled, and barked her orders into a microphone strapped around her chin.

One early morning, the drill sergeant was detailing the virtual biking scene with the usual upbeat background instrumental music bouncing off the room's walls. "OK, it is early morning as we ride on this smooth, paved road facing the glowing eastern mountains, barely hiding the coming morning sun. Look to the pasture to the right and note the galloping thoroughbreds keeping pace with us."

I looked to the right and saw a two-hundred-pound newcomer already panting as he pedaled away. I was glad to see another male in the class and nodded with a smile. Sergeant Mean continued, "We are now entering the foot-hills, so let's crank the resistance a couple more rounds." I followed orders and turned the knob two revolutions, but noticed the newcomer rotated his hand without making contact with his knob. I took a mental note, in case the "foothills" turned into "mountains." It did not take long.

"The slope is getting steeper as we now see the orange morning sun peering over the mountains," she announced, asking for three more cranks of the resistance knob. "And listen to the waterfall feeding the brook on the left of the road." The newcomer and I were doing our part for the audio effect with our dropping beads of sweat. "We now feel the warmth of the morning sun and we could sure use that western wind at our backs as this road steepens. Perhaps the new guy in the back in the Purdue shirt could dismount and turn on the fan." The newcomer was not wearing a Purdue shirt, so I dutifully began my dismount, looking over my shoulder at the fan on the back wall. But my right foot was caught in the pedal strap and held there tightly as the rest of my frame crashed into the floor with a resounding *thud*. I ended up on my back as my right foot finally released from the pedal strap.

"Omigosh! Are you OK, Mr. Purdue?" the sergeant implored, showing the first sign of compassion I had seen in two weeks. All eyes were on me now, awaiting my response. Once again, I was in a situation where I had a very short time to provide effective communication, in this case to minimize humiliation. I snapped up from the floor, not making any eye contact, and while making my way with a slight limp toward the fan, I responded loudly above the music, "I'm fine, I just hit a chuckhole!"

And while many find texting and emailing an efficient way to communicate, I found a way to stumble there as well. After coaching Dagney's NJB and All Net teams for four years I decided it was time to get another voice between us. I hired Aimee, a former Division I player to provide one on one training for Dagney and some of her teammates during the summer months. I told Aimee that I would be considering her for the team's coaching position if the summer training went well. After observing several training sessions from the corner of the gym I decided that Aimee would be a good coach and decided to start the conversation. Sitting in my back yard one Friday evening with Dana and my laptop I decided to send her an email.

*Hi Aimee, hope you are having a good Friday. I have been watching you and I have to say I am very impressed with your fundamentals. I think it is time we get together. Perhaps you could recommend a time and place?*

OK, so how many "Aimee's" could I have in my predictive text memory? Turned out I must have done a "reply all" to a St. Mary's email once because five minutes later I got a reply from Aimee, a St. Mary's mother.

*Charlie, I have to say I am quite taken by your email. Did you mean it for me?*

The reply email I sent to the only other Aimee I knew on the planet was the fastest words per minute I typed in my life.

So what does this unfortunate history of mine have to do with timeouts? Communication under duress. The beautiful game of hoops is a game of streaks. As a coach, you have to call timeout early in the opposition's streak in order to try to change the momentum. You are challenged to come up with your strategy while coaching the action on the floor, and then you have only sixty seconds to effectively communicate your change to ten-year-old girls, to try to turn loss to victory.

I have always been sensitive to my breath at timeouts and tried to use breath mints when coaching the girls, motivated by some miserable timeouts in high school. I remember my high school coach in my face at a timeout toward the end of the game, his mouth dried from three quarters of screaming, expelling his bad breath. If I cringed at all he would only scream louder and closer. Then there was Dan, a senior forward during my junior year, who experimented for a couple games by chewing a clove of garlic to weaken his defender. While Dan sometimes successfully cleared out the middle with his drives, it made timeouts reek and Dick, our star forward, hold his nose. Dan went on to be a successful lawyer, so I am sure he learned good oral hygiene.

One timeout that comes to mind was during Casey's fifth-grade game against St. Lucy's at Howley Hall. We were down by one point; Lucy's had the ball with 30 seconds left. The gym was loud this night, so I popped a mint just prior to raising my hands in the "T" formation for the ref to give our last timeout. As always, I asked the five girls in the game to gather around me in a circle. "OK, they have the sub, number 14, guarding Casey, so let's switch Caitlin to point and get the ball to Casey on the wing."

"Number 14 SO can't stop you, Casey," interrupted Andrea. Forty-nine seconds and counting, and Christina followed with, "Who took my water?"

"Never mind the water, we need to change our defense to-"

Again I was interrupted with, "Casey, that's MY water!"

"No, look, it's got my initials on it." Forty seconds.

"Forget the water!" I yelled. "There are only thirty seconds left anyway! We are changing to our half-court trap zone." I thought I had their attention.

"I smell a mint, peppermint," remarked Kelsey.

"Kelsey, you are going to play the middle on the trap."

"Who's got the mint?" Kelsey would not let it go.

"Not me, I don't like peppermint." Casey this time.

"Forget the mint!" I demanded.

"It's not peppermint, it smells like spearmint," added Amanda.

Twenty-one seconds.

"Look, I have the mint and it's peppermint, can we talk about the trapping zone?" I'm pleading now.

"Do you have an extra mint, coach?"

"After the game! Now, here's how we are going to align for the zone, Andrea ... "

"I thought we were playing man-to-man," posed Andrea.

"Yes, but now we are switching to the trapping zone."

BUZZZZZZZZZZZZZZZ!

"Ref, that can't be sixty seconds!" I begged.

"Blue ball out, Coach, take a seat."

We lost the game by one point but most of the girls went home with fresh peppermint breath.

Another timeout with Sydney's fifth-grade team comes to mind. The game was up for grabs in the final seconds, and I had sixty seconds to try to be concise and clear about how we were going to change our defense. (At this age it is easier to coach defense than offense.) In this case there were no questions about water or mints; in fact, I had the amazing full attention of all five girls for forty-five seconds. At that point I finished and asked, "Any questions?"

Nicole raised her hand asking, "Do we press if we score?"

"No, let's just pick them up at mid court," I responded. "Any other questions?" Four-foot-nine-inch Lauren raised her hand. "Yes, Lauren."

"In an NBA game where there are thousands of screaming fans, how do the players hear the referee's whistle?"

"Ah, they just do, Lauren … "

BUZZZZZZZZZZZZZZZ! Lauren did not participate in the changed defense.

At least Lauren's question during the precious sixty seconds that time was basketball-related. I recall a fifth-grade St. Mary's game with that same team against St. Justin's. St. Justin's was a formidable competitor, and having never beaten them with the St. Mary's boys' team and Casey's team, I was very pumped up about revenge with Sydney's talented fifth-grade team.

St. Justin's had a very tall center by the name of Amanda. Today Amanda is a six-foot-six star on the UCLA volleyball team; that night she was the most intimidating figure my girls had ever seen. We were only down 14-13 and had the ball with fifty seconds to go. I called timeout to set up the last play for our best shooting guard, Kate (in later years, my trainer). Kristin, our tallest girl at five feet seven (who went on to play high school and college hoops) had held Amanda scoreless, but Amanda with her height had also contained Kristin. I wanted to set up a play where Kate came off a pick from Alexandra and took a pass from Danica. I had it all in my mind when I called the timeout, had the girls gathered in the circle and began marking on my board. I looked up at my tired fifth graders and began spelling out the plan when I noticed Lauren was gazing away from the circle, her thoughts clearly not on the game. As one of my best players, she was in the game at the time and I needed her complete focus. When I finished my first pass at the play I asked if there were any questions. Silence. I asked a second time looking straight at Lauren as I knew she had not grasped the play. Her deep brown eyes met mine and I could see she was succumbing to my pressure for a question. I was glad to see her finally raise her hand, thinking perhaps she was getting her head back into the game at this critical juncture. "Yes, Lauren, what part of the play do you not understand? What is your question?"

"Coach," she responded, "Why is the nickel larger than the dime?"

"Lauren, let's discuss later. Kate ... "

"The dime is worth twice the nickel, so why is the nickel bigger?" Alexandra (who was supposed to set the pick) responded.

"Alexandra, after Kate throws the ball in to Danica, you need to set a pick on the basket side for Kate ... " I interrupted.

"Yeah, like the nickel is larger than the penny and smaller than the quarter like it's supposed to be," added Sydney. "So why is it bigger than the dime? You know, like the quarter is smaller than the fifty cent piece ... "

"Girls, PLEASE, forget the nickel for now. Kate, you need to ... "

BUZZZZZZZZZZZZZZZ!

Independent of any coaching from me, Sydney was ready to take a shot, but was staring at six-foot Amanda. In a complete state of horror, she dished the ball off to Kate, who dropped in a ten-footer with thirty seconds to go, to win 15-14. To the parents, it looked like the timeout worked. Fact is, good players like Kristin and Kate make good coaches, even after dysfunctional timeouts.

In another fourth-grade club game, I called timeout to figure out a way to stop a tall, talented girl who was dominating us. This girl was four inches taller than any of our girls and she was at least two years ahead of all of them in physical maturity. I turned to my tallest girl, assigned with her defense, though a full head shorter than her dominant opponent, and asked, "Can you front her, Stephanie?"

"No!"

"I think you can, why don't you think you can?"

"She's too fat! She pushes me and I'm like falling down," she screamed.

"Honey, we don't call girls fat, that's not nice."

"My mother says girls like that are not fat, just plus-sized models," Dagney chimed in.

"What?"

"Plus-sized models. We have a cat named Denzel that Dad calls a lazy, fat cat but I call it a plus-sized model cat because Dad hurt its feelings," Dagney explained to the now completely focused circle of girls.

"OK, Stephanie, front the plus-sized model," I implored.

"I can't, I can't stop the plus-sized girl!"

BUZZZZZZZZZZZZZ!

"*OCCD, OCCD, OCCD!*"

All my girls have been sweethearts, but in the heat of battle they can say uncharacteristic things, such as Stephanie regarding the plus-sized model. I did my best to teach the girls character as well as basketball. The "team" concept is an overused term, but if there ever was a sport that required true teamwork, it is hoops. I emphasized that teammates have to be no different than best friends. If you had a disagreement or conflict with a teammate you did not talk about it behind her back, nor did you make an emotional scene in front of the rest of the team (e.g. Lauren's "precision" pot shot at Sydney during the vocabulary lesson). No, you took up issues with your teammate on a one-to-one basis, and I would be there to help if needed.

During another timeout, as I was delivering my message with all the girls surrounding me in a circle, I was interrupted by Lauren. "Coach?" I ignored her and kept trying to communicate how we were not "helping" on number 21.

"Ashley, your girl is not involved in the offense, so why aren't you picking up number 21 when she beats Kate to the paint?"

"I can't guard her, she's frightening."

"Frightening, why?"

"She looks like a boy."

"Coach?" Lauren again. I once again tried to ignore her, but made the mistake of making eye contact and she seized the opportunity with, "Coach, would now be a good time to like take it up one-on-one with Sydney on like how she like hogs the ball and never passes to me when I am always wide open?"

BUZZZZZZZZZZZ!

*"OCCD, OCCD, OCCD! Serenity Now!"*

When girls begin playing hoops for the first time, they really do get caught up in the heat of battle. Timeouts are always tough, but when the game gets a little physical, timeouts can turn into a series of emotional outbursts.

One of Sydney's games against St. Andrews was getting very physical. I had already taken out two crying girls . Down on one knee in the middle of a circle of eight girls during timeout, I decided to communicate eye to eye to my fifth-grade team. "Sydney, Meghann, why did you not execute the high-low when Danica called it out? You both stayed on the baseline."

Sydney responded, honestly as always, "Dad, I forgot which girl goes high and which girl goes low."

"Five is higher than four so five goes," Meghann, who was playing four, correctly pointed out.

"OK, they switched to man-to-man, so let's set up a pick and roll off Danica's dribble." Lindsey was in my face with her bright blue eyes, waving her hand. "Yes, Lindsey."

"Danica keeps bossing me around."

"Lindsey, Danica is the point guard, she directs the offense."

"But she's not the boss of me!"

"Lindsey, listen up. Girls, number 33 was wide open. Lindsey, aren't you supposed to guard her?"

"I was, Coach, but now I'm guarding 53."

"No, KATE is guarding 53."

"I don't want to guard 33, she has bad breath!"

"Coach, you could give her one of your mints."

"Lindsey … "

BUZZZZZZZZZZZZZZ!

A business associate, Craig Shields, discovered how a ten year old mind wants to do anyting possible to help a coach during a timeout.  In this case, it was a ten year old boy and the following excerpt from Craig's blog http://craigshieldsquestions.com/coaching-another-anecdote/ captures the moment.

*I coached 5<sup>th</sup>grade boys basketball at the school a couple of years ago. It goes without saying that kids at this level can,* *under the pressure of a game situation, forget everything we've worked on and do… whatever.*

*Leading by nine points in a game with two minutes left, I called a full time out and told the team, "Look. We're way ahead. The only way we can lose this game is if we panic, and throw the ball away. Take CARE of the ball. Move without the ball on offense, get open, pass it around. Shoot if you have an easy shot, but ONLY if you have an easy shot."*

*Well, we lost the ball a couple of times, and some kid put the icing on the cake with an off-balance 20-foot airball. With 90 seconds to go, our lead was cut to THREE points.*

*Time out — again.*

*"Look," I said. "Do you see all those people up in the stands? All the parents and grandparents and aunts and uncles? If we lose a nine point lead in final two minutes in front of all those people, I'm going to be so embarrassed that I'm going to want to jump off a bridge. By the way," I said, "I'm kinda new around here. Are there any REALLY TALL bridges I could jump off?"*

*One of the kids, who couldn't have weighed more than about 60 pounds, shot up his hand. "Oh yes, coach, yes! There's a **huge** bridge right outside town!"*

*I laughed. He just wanted to help.*

Communicating with fifth-grade girls is challenging enough, and the sixty-second constraint nearly made my efforts hopeless. But I have to admit that over the years I got better. Through a lot of hits and misses, I actually learned how to communicate with the girls at their level. Perhaps even more helpful was listening to their conversations among themselves, which could be amazing.

Gyms have been a precious commodity in the Silicon Valley, and sometimes I had to drive the girls to the CT English middle school gym in the Santa Cruz Mountains. This gave me a great opportunity to listen to the six girls in Dana's Yukon, chucking it up. During one memorable trip with the Los Gatos All Net club team, the conversation went something like this.

Girl one: "Yesterday I saw like the most scary movie. It was like this girl was sitting up in her bed, and like the wind was blowing and like her head was going around in circles just like my doll, and then she started screaming and like throwing up all over herself."

Girl two: "Ooooh, weird, what was the name of the movie?"

Girl one: "The Exodus."

Girl three: "I used to get scared at scary movies, but now I don't."

Girl four: "How come you don't get scared?"

Girl three: "Because now I just like talk out loud and say something funny, like 'doesn't that guy look funny with that knife in his head, hehehehe…'"

Girl five to girl two: "Did your sister go to the St. Andrew's dance last night?"

Girl two: "Yeah."

Girl five: "Did she slow dance with Ryan?"

Girl two: "Yeah."

Girl five: "Did his hands feel like sandpaper?"

Girl two: "She said they felt like wet lizards."

Girl one to group: "My friend Angela threw up on my back during science yesterday."

All girls: "oooooo, gross!"

Girl three, pointing out the window: "Los Gatos has a lot of those like wooden houses with those like shutters and those post thingies on the porch."

Girl six: "My mom said they are a special design, I think she said Victorian secret."

Girl five to girl six: "How come your house still has the Christmas lights up?"

Girl six: "My mom yelled at my dad yesterday and told him to get off his butt and take them down."

Girl one to girl six: "What did he say?"

Girl six: "He said, 'OK honey, I will stop my job, my career, and my entire life this weekend and take down the lights!'"

Girl three to group: "Where are we going to put our trophies on the flight back from the tournament this weekend? They'll be too big for my bag."

While I don't deliver a timeout message in the "like" language, I have learned to use analogies that young girls can relate to. When I told Sydney she needed to put more arch on her free throw and not dispense the ball like a Pez dispenser, she really understood and even put some back-spin on her shot.

The most important lesson for timeouts is to keep the message simple and don't try to fix the whole game in sixty seconds. The coach must communicate the single most important point to help the girls win. Looking back at ineffective timeouts, I have to say that the experience of failing to communicate the key message during the precious sixty-second slices of time helped to diffuse my overly competitive nature and my OCCD affliction. Coming home, especially after a loss, reflecting on the failed time-outs and laughing about it was the best medicine to deal with my OCCD.

# 7

## GAMES

*"We can't win at home. We can't win on the road. As general manager, I just can't figure out where else to play."*

–Pat Williams, Orlando Magic general manager, on his team's 7-27 record in 1992

Coaching basketball turned out to be not that different emotionally than actually playing the game. Practices can get so old and even dreadful, but on game day you feel the excitement and tingling in the stomach hours before the tip (if you have OCCD).

Another confession I have to make now is how I scheduled my work around games. As soon as the season's schedule was established, I entered it into my work calendar and in later years into my Outlook calendar. I scheduled any meetings around the games; I tried to get business traveling out of the way just prior to the season and then let it stack up to the week after the season. As a VP of Sales, I fabricated customer visits or meetings in my Outlook schedule that matched game times, which automatically did not allow others to schedule me into meetings. Mind you, these were important meetings. I once moved a trade association conference to accommodate a sixth-grade tournament. My most embarrassing confession is that I manipulated Board of Directors meetings around games with lame excuses, including meetings that required directors to travel into town. I can accurately say that I have missed only one game of a team I coached in sixteen years of coaching. So to my bosses, fellow directors, colleagues and subordinates, I hereby come clean. I could come up with something lame like, "It was for the good of the girls," but that would not be true, as I always had excellent assistant coaches. Fact is, it was for the good of me and my OCCD affliction. I am not proud of my deception, but at least I am admitting my sickness, this addiction. I hope you find it in your hearts to understand.

Earlier, I confessed that for a while I kept track of my won-lost record as a girls' teams coach. The sad truth is that I also remember most of the games, and especially turning points in the games or memorable moments. My only defense for remembering game details while forgetting robot customers' names is that third, fourth and fifth-grade girls' games have low scores to begin with, especially fifth-grade school teams with most girls playing hoops for the first time in their lives.

I remember Casey's first fifth-grade game at St. Lawrence Academy, just off Lawrence Expressway in San Jose. The gym was small and so was the crowd, maybe one parent per child. Caroline (now a senior at SMU) got the first basket of the season to put us up 2-0 by the end of the first quarter. It was an eight-footer just to the right of the key. Casey got a lay-up at the start of the fourth quarter to put us up 8-4, and that was the final score. Who would not remember a game like that? I remember other key shots from four years of that team, such as Lauren's (trainer Kate's older sister) baseline jumper in the seventh-grade Cabrini tournament that gave us a 21-19 championship win on Super Bowl Sunday, 2001. I remember in detail the four three-pointers scored in the four years of that team; two of them well beyond the arch, desperation shots by Sheena at Sacred Heart, and Caitlin #2 from half court at St. Frances Cabrini, to send the game into an overtime that we won. Casey's team got to double digits in sixth grade and reached the thirties a couple times before they graduated eighth grade. Two years behind, Sydney's team scored a little more than Casey's. As more girls began to play club sports, by the time Dagney played fifth-grade basketball this year, games regularly reached the twenties and beyond. What a difference ten years has made in fifth-grade girls' hoops skills. There were no girls' sports at all in Indiana and many other states in the 60s, and now girls can start playing soccer at age four and hoops at age five, at Calvary. The higher scoring levels today make it easy to create annoying team stats like those in pro sports, stats with a keen grasp on the obvious, you know, like the Lakers were 24-1 this year when leading by more than twenty going into the fourth quarter.

Here are my stats. Charlie's fifth-grade St. Mary's teams were 6-0 when leading opponents by more than six points at halftime. Charlie's fifth-grade St. Mary's teams were 9-0 when holding the opponents to less than six points. Charlie's fifth-grade St. Mary's teams were 11-0 when leading by more than six points with two minutes left in the game ... Those annoying stats extend well beyond hoops and into baseball and football. There seems to be way too much data and time on the hands of sportswriters. My all time favorite basketball stat was cited by Doug Collins:

"Any time Detroit scores more than a hundred points and holds the other team below a hundred points, they almost always win."

For St. Mary's teams, I usually did not spend time on a game plan other than making sure my best defenders guarded their best offensive players, and making a rough substitution plan to ensure fair playing time. In the past year at St. Mary's, one of the mothers, Joanne, did a great job as a bench coach, substituting per the plan while I coached. It was not easy, with ten players and only twenty-four game minutes. Casey's eighth-grade school team posed serious challenges with thirteen girls. For this, I created an Excel program and substitution plan that my good friend and assistant coach, Dr. Paul, executed from the bench. If a parent complained about playing time I invited them to look at the Excel spreadsheet game plan that calculated % of game participation—or better yet, take it up with Dr. Paul. One word of advice for fathers coaching daughters - even if your daughter is the next Lisa Leslie you better make sure she spends her fair time on the bench.

The only other preparation for a school game was to pick a theme or slogan to fire the girls up. By the eighth grade some legitimate rivalries developed. So maybe before a Sacred Heart game it might be, "Let's break some hearts!" Or before a Queen of Apostles game, "Let's kick some queen!", a battle cry originated by fellow St. Mary's coach Truman. That kind of banter is OK among us friendly Catholics in the San Jose Diocese ... *I think.*

For the NJB All Net games, the assistant coach and I would develop a serious game plan. All Net is serious hoops, and I have to confess that I attended games of upcoming teams on the schedule to scout. Actually, I only did it a few times, as it became very uncomfortable. Imagine two All Net fifth-grade teams playing in a spacious high school gym. Nearly all the seats are empty, of course, as there are one or two parents and maybe a sibling per player. In the entire gym, there might be thirty fans. Then in walks a guy (me) in a sweatshirt, Purdue cap and sun shades, with a notebook and pen. This guy does not join any of the thirty fans and chooses a seat by himself away from the rest of the crowd. (This happened with me not so long ago.) As the game began, I was taking some notes when I slowly began to sense eyes on me. Looking over at the parents, I saw more and more people staring at me. I was beginning to spend more time watching the stands, as one parent leaned over to another and then both were looking at me. I became very uncomfortable, and at halftime decided to get the hell out of there, picking up my pace as I got to the door. Looking over my shoulder, I spotted two dads looking through the gym doors, and I picked up my pace even more as I got to the parking lot and close to my car. A gust of wind blew off my cap but I left it; there are many Purdue engineers in the Valley and they would not be able to trace it to me. I realized at that point there is a fine line, perception wise, between a girls' All Net scout and a child predator.

Game day at St. Mary's with my players is not the same as it was for me at St. Peter's in the 60s. I remember looking at the clock the entire day, counting the minutes until we would be on the court for that opening tip. I think my St. Mary's girls look at the clock on game day, not with anticipation for the game, but for recess. Nonetheless, St. Mary's has a cool tradition where the student hoops players wear their yellow and blue jerseys to school, over their standard uniforms, on game days.

A nice tradition that many of the Catholic grade schools have is the pre-game prayer. Girls, coaches and

even referees form a circle holding hands as the host athletic director says the "Our Father" prayer. This can serve
as preventive health care for coaches suffering from
OCCD.

I get no better feeling than when the buzzer goes off for
the tip-off. The girls are excited, I'm excited, and the
parents (at least most of them) are excited. I have both
great memories and not-so-good memories from games.

When I first started coaching Casey's fifth-grade team, I
was still in the advanced stages of OCCD. Being a competitor and an optimist, I would fantasize about the
upcoming game at the office that day or on the drive to
the gym. I remember one of my first games at St. Mary's
against the fifth graders of St. Justin's, our bitter rival. I had
just taught the girls a tip-off play at the prior practice, one
that we used in high school when we were confident of
getting the tip. One guard lines up at the tip-off circle but
takes off toward our basket when the ref tosses the ball in
the air. Our girl tips the ball to her teammate on the circle
on our side of the court. That girl pivots and passes the
ball to the streaking guard, already in the lane at free throw
depth, and the passer rushes down the middle. Most of the
time, the streaking guard would get an open lay-up. If the
defensive safety picks up the streaking guard, the passing
girl is open for the lay-up in the middle of the lane. We
practiced the drill twenty times during practice and
Andrea made the pass to Casey who made the lay-up
eighteen times, so we were ready!

I fantasized about going up 2-0 in the first five seconds
on the drive to the gym. That would be so intimidating to

Justin's, and would give our girls an early boost of confidence. I just love successful tip-off plays. At the gym I watched St. Justin's warming up, as usual looking for any left-handers, and noticed no girl who could out-tip our Kelsey. We were set when the buzzer blew for the tip-off.

As planned, Kelsey leaped up and tipped the ball toward Andrea. Andrea aggressively grabbed it and pivoted toward our basket, looking for the streaking Casey. Just as aggressively, a Justin's girl leaped toward Andrea, causing her to lead Casey a little too much on the pass. Casey reached for the ball but stumbled, kicking the ball toward our bench and hard into Janelle's nose. The ref whistled Justin's ball and I tended the teary-eyed Janelle. I remarked to Coach Paul that it makes a difference when there are defenders on the tip-off play, as I left my fantasy world and came back to fifth-grade girls' reality.

Refereeing games at this age is a real challenge. At the fifth-grade level, a serious portion of the game is spent with girls lying on the floor with arms wrapped around the ball for tie-ups. And I have had a few hackfests over the years. One of Casey's games comes to mind. Every timeout was a litany of transgressions cited from my girls about the opposing girls. At one fourth quarter timeout an animated Casey kicked off a round of reported atrocities with, "Dad, 21 poked her elbow right in my neck like this!" as she thrust her elbow into my neck, knocking me back against the wall and sending pain down my back.

"That's nothing, 14 kicked me in the knee and now it really hurts!" added Caitlin #1. (*Here we go …* )

"32 tripped me and then she laughed at me. She hurted my feelings …"

"That's nothing, the girl with the big teeth bit my arm!"

"She didn't bite you!" I challenged.

"Yes she did! It was like her mouth was open and like my elbow went in it … and then she bit me!"

"11 slapped me and called me a slut."

"11 did what?"

BUZZZZZZZZZZZ! Another wasted timeout …

That whole first year of coaching Casey's fifth-grade St. Mary's team had me fired up. I remember an early season game at St. Martins where the score was close at the beginning of the third quarter. The St. Martins girls were bringing the ball down the court toward our waiting defense. Suddenly my number 3 girl jogged over to the bench and stopped in front of me.

"Honey, get back out there, your girl is open!" I yelled. She stayed in front of me with a concerned frown. "What's wrong?" I asked, with my eyes on her open girl about to get the ball.

"I just remembered that I did not take my dog for a walk before we left for the game."

"You what?" I responded, as I now saw her unguarded girl with the ball.

"I need to go home and walk my dog so that he does not go to the bathroom on our carpet. I will be in big trouble with my mom." I watched her girl get a basket.

"Timeout!" I called out to the ref, as I put in a sub and located my frowning player's mother to deal with the dog hygiene issue.

One of that team's more memorable games was a road game at Sacred Heart that turned into a foul-plagued, grind-it-out game, another hackfest. Like most Catholic school games in the Bay Area, Sacred Heart ran a very organized venue, with an adult teacher running the score clock and one student next to the clock keeper who kept the scorebook up to date. In this particular game there was a young black-haired boy, probably an eighth grader, keeping books at the end next to our bench. In the first quarter I asked him how many timeouts I had in the first half. He looked at me in silence. In the second quarter I asked him how many fouls number 36 had on Sacred Heart. Once again he gazed at me in silence. Toward the end of the second quarter, when our Sheena got called for a foul, I asked him how many she had. Silent gaze again.

Sheena was an excellent athlete who went on to play Division I volleyball. She was very low key, soft spoken if she said anything at all, and in this Sacred Heart hackfest she fouled out early in the third quarter. Presumably, the black-haired boy silently showed Sheena's total fouls in his book to the referee. She quietly took her seat on the bench with her fifth foul and the game tied. The referee called a Sacred Heart girl for traveling right in front of Sheena, who suddenly spurted out, "Well, good to see you've got another call besides FOUL in that whistle!"

It was the most enunciation I had ever heard from Sheena. The ref swirled around, ready to call a technical foul, and with a cringe I quickly countered, "Good call ref, Sheena's just being silly, ha, ha, ha." No T. It was the closest I, or my team, ever got to receiving a technical foul.

Two more girls fouled out on our team, and with two minutes to go in the game Genna picked up her third foul. The young scorekeeper at the official's bench, who had not said a word through the whole game, turned to me with an animated, articulate voice and said with a nice smile, "That's three fouls on number 4, Coach."

Duh. I wondered what brought on that sudden use of vocal cords. Perhaps I had witnessed a Catholic miracle for the gift of speech. The game went on; they fouled out more than we did and we barely won. But the thing I remember most about the game was the sudden communication from two quiet participants.

It is sometimes difficult to get into the minds of young girls in game situations. After several practices and a few games under their belts, a coach assumes they understand the basics and are into the game situations, just as you are. But they are not always clicked in. During a fourth-grade recreational league game, Kate, one of my best players (and later my trainer), was dribbling at the point and suddenly just tucked the ball under her arm and broke for the paint like a football running back, toward a seam she saw in the zone defense. It was not until she ran eight steps and scored a basket that the startled ref blew the whistle and called traveling. Kate never changed her expression and played the rest of the quarter at point, dribbling within the rules and scoring two baskets in a row at the end of the quarter. I decided not to even take up the first-and-ten run with her at the quarter break.

I found there are times you just don't talk to girls at all. In an NJB Fourth Grade All Star tournament opener,

Dagney hit five straight field goals and two free throws. The other coach called a timeout and Pat, our assistant coach, advised me to leave Dagney at the end of the bench where she was drinking water and checking out a candy wrapper. I talked to the rest of the girls at the other end of the bench briefly and sent them all out to the court. Dagney got up to join them and proceeded to hit three more baskets to seal the win against a very good team. It was one of many sound tips Pat has given me over three years of coaching together.

Sydney had a teammate, Meghann, who never changed expression in the game, or in practice for that matter. Meghann was tall and I played her at the low post. In a game against St. Andrew's, she picked up the ball a good eighteen feet from the goal, turned toward the basket, and hit the only long shot she ever even tried playing for me. But instead of running to the defensive end with her other four teammates she ran straight to the bench and stopped, looking down at me. With a rare smile under her pretty and wide open eyes, she asked, "Coach, was that a three?"

"Meghann, get down the court, your girl is open."

"Coach, I think it was a three!"

Realizing Meghann was in a zone, I calmed down, murmured "OCCD" internally and said, "Yeah, it was a three. I'll talk to the ref about it at the end of the quarter since they only gave you two. Get down the court, 'cause your girl is about to get a two."

"Thanks Coach," she replied, and trotted down to the defensive end where her girl just air balled a wide-open five-footer. Meghann is now a Division I water polo player.

There are unique moments that only a Catholic school fifth-grade team can have. We all have seen the fans waving their arms behind the basket for opposing free throw shooters, from the high school through pro levels. The Catholic leagues, at least those around San Jose, teach the kids good game manners and distracting gestures are usually not executed during opposing free throws. Usually; I do recall a fifth-grade girls' game at St. Lucy's, when the St. Lucy's girl lined up to shoot two free throws late in the game when we led by only one point. As she lined up her first shot, I noticed a flurry of activity out of the corner of my eye at the end of my bench, within view of the shooter from St. Lucy's. Our number 89 at the end of the bench was furiously blessing herself repeatedly, mumbling, *"In the name of the Father and the Son and the Holy Spirit, Amen! In the name of the Father and the Son and the Holy Spirit, Amen! In the name of ... "* Unlike the St. Mary's girl who struggled with the Lord's Prayer, number 89 was getting it right. She was faster than the guy in the old FedEx commercial and about to throw her arm out of joint. Her St. Mary's teammate sitting in the next position leaned away from her in fear of catching one of her skinny elbows, which would have been worse than any elbow protecting a rebound.

In the midst of what was now a distraction, the St. Lucy's girl bounced the ball off the front of the rim and glanced again at our bench. Number 89 took a breather while the ref looked at her, then he turned to hand the ball to the Lucy girl for the chance to tie. As she lined up her shot, our prayer girl once again broke into her sequence, this time showing excellent ambidextrous skills as she rested her tired right arm and went aggressively into blessing mode with her left hand, hitting the forehead, chest, and shoulders with high velocity and repeatability. The Lucy girl was now one of ten girls and two referees watching number 89. But what could the ref do at a Catholic school game? Whether any Catholic player, ref, or fan believed God would answer number 89's prayers by providing another brick shot, how could anyone interrupt such fervent prayer? The Lucy girl shot another brick high off the backboard above the rim and we ended up winning by one. I thought about giving number 89 the game MVP award but decided to leave well enough alone.

The Catholic politeness of girls' school basketball during free throws seemed to wear off by the time they reached eighth grade. Another game that remains in my memory banks forever was against Sacred Heart in a tournament game. Sacred Heart has a history of wonderful volunteer coaches, but on this night they had a young coach who had an unfortunate affliction of OCCD at a young age. Unlike the fifth-grade number 89 previously discussed, he would not engage in prayer but would yell "BOX OUT!" at the top of his lungs just as our girls were releasing their free throws. Good referees would have called him on it as inappropriate for eighth-grade girls' basketball, but not this night. After he did it the second time, I politely asked him to refrain but got no response. Then, when our Caitlin #1 was releasing her first of two, he yelled again, "ANGIE SWITCH WITH ANNA NEXT SHOT!" Caitlin's shot rammed the front of the rim. The ref got the loose ball and handed it to Caitlin, and as she brought the ball back for her second shot, he yelled, "BLOCK OUT THE SHOOTER!"

Caitlin had stopped the ball motion and tucked it in at her side. She turned toward the coach with her glowing hazel eyes and yelled at the top of her lungs, "SHUT YOUR FAT MOUTH, COACH!" Our bench broke into hysterics, including her dad, Assistant Coach Paul, as one ref asked Caitlin to shoot her second shot. She made the shot and scowled at the now-stunned coach as she trotted to the defensive end. He didn't yell again the rest of the night; in fact, he rarely left his seat on the bench. Caitlin #1 is now a senior at the University of Colorado and I fully expect her to break any glass ceiling constraining her career.

I mentioned earlier that the beauty of fifth-grade girls basketball is that any girl can score, and even become a heroine. I had one girl on a fifth-grade St. Mary's team who had not scored in the first seven games. It was troubling me as we neared the end of the season. I played her extensively in the eighth game, and by the third quarter we ran into good fortune when she was fouled on a lay-up and made her first basket of the year. She lined up for the free throw to get a chance for the three-point play. Now for some background, I have taught all my girls the importance of concentration on free throws. I tell them that in the heat of a close game, opposing fans (or in the earlier case, the Sacred Heart coach) will do anything they can to distract you from making the shot. So as not to be distracted, I encourage them to come up with their own focused sequence for shooting free throws, while offering them mine as an example:

1.   Line up the right foot with the basket to minimize the distance from your shooting shoulder to the hoop.
2.   Leave the toe about half an inch from the shooting line.
3.   Bounce the ball three times.
4.   Find the valve and put the middle finger on the seam below the valve.
5.   Take a deep breath and concentrate on the back of the rim.
6.   Visualize your shot falling through the rim.
7.   Bend the knees.
8.   Shoot the shot from the fingers.
9.   Wave goodbye to the shot when it leaves the fingers, to ensure backspin.
10. Don't celebrate when it goes in; act like it has happened before (for my fifth-grade girls).

Now back to the fifth grader who is about to shoot her first free throw, ever. When the referee handed her the ball, she fumbled it into the paint and number 13 on St. Andrews picked it up and handed it back to her. The referee rightfully intervened, took the ball and handed it back to our newly found scorer. She took four dribbles, lined up her shot, took a deep breath and promptly banked in the free throw for her third point of the game, of the season, and of her life. Three trips down the floor later, she was fouled on a missed shot attempt, this time getting two free throws. Number 13 of St. Andrews picked up the loose ball, handed it to the referee who then handed it to our scorer, and she once again banked in her free throw after repeating the four-dribble ritual. The other ref got the loose ball and bounced it to the second ref, who then handed it to our four-point scorer. She then handed the ball to number 13 of St. Andrews, who politely handed it back to the same ref, who forgivingly handed it back to our shooter, who then banked in her fifth and final point of the season. At the end-of-season party, I asked her why she handed the ball to number 13 and found out that she was simply following my advice to keep the same sequence for shooting free throws, as number 13 had handled the ball each of the previous shots.

I wondered if that was it, or if she was superstitious. Anyone who follows professional sports knows that many athletes are superstitious. Baseball players step over the baseline when retreating to the dugout each inning, wear the same dirty socks every day while on a hitting streak, etc. There is nothing wrong with a little superstition among fifth-grade basketball girls.

I always tried to keep the bench involved in the game. One example was having the bench countdown the seconds at the end of quarters when we had the ball so the girls on the floor did not have to look at the clock. Another example was with Dagney's St. Mary's team where I had a play to make a high pass to our tallest forward, Molly. It was the grade school version of the "alley-oop" play. Our point guard called out "Hi Molly!" and

Molly would position herself with her arms up for the pass. If she collected the pass and scored, the bench completed the play by yelling in unison, "How are you Molly?" I have to confess we did not execute the full dialogue very often.

As discussed earlier, much more time is available at practices than those precious game minutes to teach girls the game of basketball. But I have always done what I could to maximize the learning experience of the game itself. If a girl make a mental error, many times I will send in a substitute for her right away. This gives me the opportunity to explain the error while the play is fresh in her mind. At the end of the discussion I put her right back into the game. I think this is much more effective than reviewing the error at the next practice or worse, taking her out of the game with no feedback at all.

Yet another game remains fixed in my mind, for most unpleasant reasons. On February 7, 2002, Casey's eighth-grade St. Mary's team was playing Holy Family in a tournament at St. Lucy's. Like so many times before, I had manipulated/fabricated my schedule to make sure I could make the early 3:45 start time. We had a familiar start, an 8-2 lead with Casey scoring six of the first eight points and an assist to Kelsey for the fourth basket after being triple teamed. After a Holy Family timeout, we had a play we saw so many times in the season, a box-and-one defense on Casey. For non-hoopsters, a box-and-one is when one defender guards the best offensive player and the others form a 2-2 box around the paint, where the closest to the target double-teams her. All five Holy Family girls were fixated on Casey and, as I had instructed her when she was double- or triple-teamed, she looked for the open girl and made the pass. Unfortunately, we missed a lot of easy shots and they began making theirs.

In the middle of the second quarter, a Holy Family girl who probably had next to no defensive training undercut Casey, who went flying into the seats. My first instinct as a father was to take her out of the game, but when she came out of the seats laughing and the fouler was crying, I chose to leave her in. We only had a four-point lead. With a minute to go in the second quarter, I watched a scene on the court that is indelible in my memory. Casey did a head fake and dribbled around her defender into the paint on her way to another lay-up. The next defender in the box simply whacked her from the side as the ball went flying out of bounds and Casey fell to the floor, screaming and grabbing her left knee. I ran onto the floor to join her. She was sobbing, saying, "Dad, I felt a big pop in my knee!" I helped her off the floor and she sat on the bench for the rest of the game. For the remainder of the game, I looked at her every time there was a dead ball on the court. She sat holding her left knee, always cheering for her St. Mary's teammates.

At the first meeting with Dr. Rollins, he said that since he felt no "float" in her knee, it might be just an MCL tear that could heal naturally. For three days I awaited the results of the MRI, praying that it was only an MCL. On the fourth day I took a call from Dr. Rollins. My stomach panged and I lost my breath when I heard the words, "Charlie, I'm sorry, but Casey tore her ACL."

I have had my own share of athletic injuries, but never suffered the pain and anguish of watching my thirteen-year-old daughter suffering in a hospital bed an hour after surgery, another memory indelibly inscribed in my memory banks. Casey tore her other ACL during her sophomore year at Archbishop Mitty High School and had a third knee surgery after her freshman year field hockey season at Northeastern University. But the guilt I hold for that first ACL has never left me to this day, as that incident was under my control. I still occasionally wake up at night asking myself why I did not take her out of the game when she was knocked into the seats. Was winning the game more important to me than her safety? My guilt only intensified when I reminded myself that we ended up winning the game without her. I wondered if my bad coaching decision cost her her dream to make it in high school and college in hoops.

My burden was lessened somewhat by Casey excelling at field hockey in high school, which led to a Division I experience at Northeastern. One positive outcome of this unfortunate event was the incredible admiration I gained, watching my daughter go through ninety minutes of rehabilitation daily for months. Her motivation to get back into sports was beyond my wildest expectations. As I observed earlier with Sydney and theater, nothing impresses a parent more than seeing their offspring do something that they themselves could never do. When I had my knee injury, I gave up organized basketball. Casey went through three knee surgeries and three rehabs. If she is as motivated in her chosen profession, she will be most successful.

Of all the experiences I had as a coach for young girls, nothing had a stronger effect on setting proper priorities than this experience with my own daughter; nothing else was as effective in mellowing my competitiveness. There is a priority for personal health. As I said earlier, girls' sports have made huge progress as far as the level of play at earlier ages—but unfortunately, so have the injuries.

# 8

## LIFE LESSONS

*"I tell kids to pursue their basketball dreams, but I tell them to not let that be their only dream."*

*- Kareem Abdul-Jabbar*

Fingerprinting to be a volunteer coach
for NJB Basketball - $10

Bag of reward candy bars - $11

Basketball marking board - $16

Replacing NJB basketball that disappeared down the driveway and into the creek - $26

Gaining lifetime friendship with three referees - Priceless? ... ... ... ... ... no, $237.

After making an overly competitive ass of myself in OCCD-relapse moments during two games in my first season, I showed up the next year with peace offerings to three refs of Purdue athletic jackets. As with the jackets issue and other experiences mentioned earlier, the life lessons have been numerous, for both the coaches and girls. But my single most important life lesson as a coach was comprehending the priorities of grade-school-age girls.

I found a recent article in *The Week*, "Washington's New Power Game," amusing. It seems that with the president's love for hoops and his regular pickup games, basketball is suddenly "in" in the nation's capital. Ironically, some of the best high school and college hoops have always surrounded the capital in the D.C./Virginia/Maryland corridor. According to former Clinton press secretary Dee Dee Myers, the hottest invite in Washington is not a state dinner but "... a pickup game with Obama. That's the inner, inner, inner sanctum."[1] These pickup games happen twice per week. All over town, more people are playing hoops, in newly started leagues, private schools and even in Congress. A man who runs a city youth training camp company was approached by a CEO who proposed a business: giving basketball lessons on Capitol Hill to Congressmen and others yearning to get close to Obama in a game.

While some girls who played for me at the club level would be qualified to compete in the president's hoops game, the thought of a Congressman suddenly learning hoops to get close to the president is entertaining. One can develop an acceptable level of golf skills by taking individual lessons and practicing at the driving range, but basketball can only be learned by playing with a *team*, in real, organized games. The inner city kids who become so skilled at hoops at a young age do not get there by buying individual lessons. They excel by playing on teams daily and developing the instincts of team basketball. However, I am happy to see the pickup-game level of hoops get national attention.

Note to any politician or lobbyist who did not play high school hoops: Our president played high school hoops. He's probably got game. Don't humiliate yourself.

The beauty of basketball (and other organized team sports) is that the players learn both physical skills and social skills, more so, in my opinion, than in the more individual sports such as golf, tennis, swimming, wrestling, etc. I will always remember the contrast between the first practices of NJB All Star or All Net teams vs. the end-of-year parties. At the first practices the young girls are highly reserved, and sit in the circle not too close to the unknown girl next to them. By the end of the season there are high fives and hugs on the floor. The bonding that happens when ten girls are faced with a common challenge on the court is no different than the collaboration they will need later in life as engineers, accountants, parents and community members.

When I put together the sales force and customer support organization at my robot company, I saw a lot of résumés. I always gave a second look to anyone, male or female, who had played team sports. Competing against global robot giants required my organization to maximize its strengths and work together as a loyal, cohesive team. I definitely saw the teamwork ethic in most of the personnel who had played organized team sports. As a small but closely-knit team, we indeed succeeded against much larger global corporate competitors.

I read a story in the *New Yorker*, "How David Beats Goliath" by Malcolm Gladwell. He wrote about an NJB coach who grew up in Mumbai with cricket and soccer—and was puzzled by the way Americans played basketball. Once a team scored, it would immediately retreat to its end and patiently wait for the other team to arrive at that end of the court. He observed that the basketball court was ninety-four feet long but the teams only contested each other for twenty-four feet of that length, with a few exceptions of a full court press at the end of games. Since his team of twelve-year-old girls was, for the most part, inexperienced in hoops, he instigated a full court defense and won his division against taller and more experienced teams. While he did not know basketball that deeply, he managed the team as he did his software company, maximizing strengths and minimizing exposure to weaknesses.

Competitive software companies, competitive twelve-year-old basketball teams: the strategy can be the same. A collection of girls playing basketball for the first time is not unlike a startup company. While you need a seasoned gray-hair for CEO (the coach) and COO (the assistant coach), you are well served to go with high energy, fast moving, agile employees who are not bogged down by traditional business processes.

I can relate so many parallels with young girls' basketball and business or other career paths, but an important one is the ethic of training, practice, and commitment. Unless you inherit your parent's business, you have to make a long-term plan to succeed, and I would submit that even those inheriting a business need to follow the ethic. You have to study, get a degree, start at the bottom of the organizational chart and work your butt off to gain promotions, one at a time. I try to teach this ethic to my girls in hoops. Some girls may have a short term advantage due to physical maturity, or have one incredible game in which they were "hot" from the field—but succeeding in hoops requires practice, practice and practice, week after week, along with setting personal goals.

Some of the most successful executives I have met have been those who had a keen grasp on what they *did not* know. They had to concentrate on improving their aptitude in these weaker areas or hire an expert smarter than them in that field. The girls I have coached know that if they get hot in one game and carry the team they are not suddenly a superstar. And I'll bet that if later in life they are in the right cubicle for the right company at the right time they will not confuse sudden financial success with unbridled brilliance.

I am a big fan of man-to-man defense for a multitude of reasons. I learned early on that the term "man-to-man" does not apply to young girls; but as one Belmar, New Jersey girls' high school coach in the 80s said, "We play man-to-man defense. Person-to-person sounds like a telephone call."

Girl-to-girl, man-to-man, whatever you want to call it, it is the way to start young kids in hoops. Too many coaches start their kids with zones. It is the tempting thing to do when the coach's only objective is winning; tempting, because most girls can't hit a shot more than ten feet from the basket at this age. If you pack the defense in a 2-1-2 zone in the paint, yeah, you probably have a better chance to win. But at the end of the year, the girls have not learned defensive skills. I would rather lose a couple games (and have) because my girls were beaten off the dribble playing man-to-man, knowing that at the end of the season they will be better at moving their feet, and ultimately better defensive athletes. And when they play zone and have to guard outside shooters they will be more successful, having learned defense playing man-to-man.

Recently I saw two fifth-grade girls' teams play in a school game. Both teams were packed in the paint with zones while the offensive team just passed around the perimeter, uncontested by the defense, as they followed the coach's orders to stay in the paint. After a while, at each end of the court, someone either made an errant pass or took a long shot and missed. Two quarters passed; I couldn't take it and left the gym. A soccer game had broken out in what was supposed to be a basketball game, except this was even less interesting than soccer. When we play teams and I see the other five girls lined up on defense in the paint with their hands in the air, I remember basketball great Norm Sloan, who also hated the zone defense, describing it as a 7-11 stick up.

The NJB division level addresses this important issue at the early age by requiring two quarters of the game to be played man-to-man and two quarters in zone. For those four quarters, each girl has to play at least two quarters. Then a "fifth quarter" is played with no playing time or defense requirements.

I like the accountability of man-to-man. There is no confusion with who is accountable for defense when a girl scores against a man-to-man. At this young age, I believe it is healthy for the girls to look to themselves and not blame someone else in the zone for the opponents' score. One of the biggest challenges any basketball coach has with fifth-grade kids—boxing out on shots—is so much easier to teach when each girl knows who she is responsible for boxing out. When one of my girl's defensive assignments gets an offensive rebound and a putback score against us, everybody knows who is accountable.

And when my player looks over to the bench at me, taps her chest and says, "My bad, coach," I yell back, "That's OK, box her out next time," smiling because my girl has taken full personal accountability at the age of eleven. That puts her ahead of many adults in accepting personal accountability.

As an aside, accountability seems to be lacking more and more, and not just with politicians and talk show hosts but also with students, teachers, parents and working professionals.

"The teacher didn't do a good job of explaining it to my daughter."

"They put the stop sign in a stupid location."

"Sorry we were late for the game but your directions were bad, Coach."

"Dana, you have more time to help her with her math than I do…"

It seems it is always someone else's fault, not the parent's, not the worker's nor the politician's. Wouldn't life be simple if accountability was as simple as "who was supposed to be guarding the girl who scored?"

It is never too early to teach integrity. The longer I operate in the business world, the more valued personal integrity has become, both in how people perceive me and in how I perceive and trust them. Integrity is accepting loss with class and personal accountability. Integrity is never taking a cheap shot at a player on the other team, personal or physical, direct or indirect. I had a long talk with Stephanie after the "plus-size model" game, about what happens when someone tags another with a slur, even if indirectly. I asked her to look ahead at the next classmate that she sees being bullied, teased or slandered, and come to their defense. Stephanie is a wonderful girl; I heard feedback that she did exactly that.

Our NJB All Net team has a history of second half comebacks. Once we were trailing by seventeen points in the first half but Sarah, Delaney and Lauren hit a combined six three-point shots, with the sixth one at six seconds left on the clock, to win by one point. This kind of three-point shooting is unheard of for girls at this age—but these girls refused to lose. We were not known as a three-point shooting team; the opposing team was devastated. (In a similar situation, our team would have been devastated as well.) Later, some of our parents overheard the other team's parents in the parking lot, trading observations regarding how all the referees' bad calls in the second half cost them the game as their girls listened.

Coaches should never allow referees to be scapegoats. The best life lesson coaches can provide when girls refer to officiating is to take the responsibility for the loss on the coaching staff. Players should only focus on the things they can control. Integrity *and* accountability …

This same team was returning to San Jose on a flight after coming in third in the All Net Nationals. I was sitting across the aisle from Nicole, who was clinging to her trophy and talking to Dagney. Nicole was a good athlete; I drafted her on every team I coached, including the fifth-grade St. Mary's team. Nicole would have been a star on the Los Gatos Recreational team, or one of the best in the league in regular NJB, yet she chose to try out for this extremely competitive and talented All Net team. She had scored some key baskets in the past season including a pivotal fifteen footer in the Silicon Valley championship. She averaged less playing time per game than I would have liked, but was sitting with the third trophy she had won that year. I leaned across the aisle and asked her, "Nicole, now that the season is over, do you wish you had played on a regular NJB team with a lot more playing time?"

Remarkably, with little hesitation, she looked at her trophy and responded, "No, Coach, I loved being part of the best team I could ever play for." I suddenly got a lump in my throat and I felt guilty that a fifth-grade girl with this kind of team attitude did not get maximum playing time.

Nicole's priorities have an interesting parallel with what kids go on to do for their life's work. They will be faced with career decisions. Is it better to work as the big dog, maybe president of a small, obscure company, or to be part of a larger team that makes history? Would it be better to have worked early on for Google, as part of a team? Would it have been better to work as a team contributor to a nonprofit organization that provided food and clothing to needy families? Given Nicole's clear priorities, I'll bet that she will be a successful part of a team that makes life better for other people.

The ethic that every coach wants is the *team* ethic. No terms have been more overused in the corporate setting than team, teamwork, team player, etc. Any human resource professional will probe for a candidate's teamwork ethic in a job interview. Any smart applicant will extol his or her teamwork ethic in the submitted résumé. However, while most employees do all they can to exercise team play in business, some make their own advancement first priority in the end. Sooner or later that personality trait becomes clear to management, which tarnishes their image and hinders them in the very advancement objective they are pursuing.

Nicole and Dagney played on the St. Mary's fifth-grade team. The two of them, along with Kate, another NJB player and Ally, got most of our points in a February 11, 2009 game against St. Andrews. All ten girls played fair if not equal time and we trailed most of the game. With ten seconds left and our five best players on the floor, we got the go-ahead basket to win 22-20. All five girls on the bench leaped up, screaming their lungs out as they raced to join the five on the floor, pounding their backs and hugging. Only one of the girls on the bench had scored, yet they all had as much exuberance for the victory as the five on the floor who clinched the win. The girls that night, especially the five from the bench made such an impression on me. There was no Terrell Owens touchdown dance by the girl who made the winning basket, and none of the self-promotion that you see too often in professional sports. It was one of the best examples of the absolute beauty of authentic team ethic. This ethic is so refreshingly genuine in fifth-grade girls basketball. On the drive home that night, I wondered how many companies would have equal exuberance from all their employees when one salesperson got the one order on the last afternoon of the quarter that made the company's numbers.

When I watch one of my fifth-grade All Net girls see her teammate about to get picked off on defense and suddenly yell "I got her" as she steps up to help, it glows with teamwork. When the girl who got picked suddenly jerks her head looking for the girl her helping teammate was guarding, finds her and picks her up, yelling "I got your girl!", it glows with teammate support. And when I see

Lauren, a good shooter on our All Net team, pass up a ten-footer to dish to Alena who is five feet closer to the rim, it warms my heart. I am seeing teamwork at its best. If only we "grownups" exhibited such teamwork and support for fellow employees, fellow teachers, fellow family members … I think my All Net girls are going to be very successful in the roles they choose in life because they will put the company, the school, the family or the team before their own needs.

Another valuable life lesson is the value of recognition and acknowledgment. While there are not enough hours in the day to cover all the advice a coach could provide girls at this age for skill improvements, it is important to mix in compliments. Positive reinforcement has even more value than the corrective comments.

As a young engineer at Monsanto's corporate engineering department, I attended several parties to honor retiring engineers, sometimes with slide shows of his career incorporating his pictures. The retiring engineer glowed with the acknowledgment he was getting from management and his peers. I realized that, for the most part, only at retirement were these guys given public recognition. I could not understand why the utmost in motivation techniques was only utilized when the receiver would no longer be working. It was analogous to a eulogy. When I was vice president of sales of a robot company, I remembered that. At every annual sales kickoff meeting, I made a slide (and later, PowerPoint presentation) that included each salesperson in a photograph or two, taken discretely by me or by fellow travelers. I would also include acknowledgment of his/her best accomplishment in the past year. Nothing motivated the sales folks more than seeing their picture on a PowerPoint presentation and hearing positive things about their year in the presence of their peers.

As with the sales force of my robotics company, I acknowledged my girls at the end-of-year team parties. I followed the example set by Casey's club soccer coach, Steve Stavis, who wrote a poem about each girl at the end of the season. I wrote limericks for each girl, citing a moment or two in the season where they made a game-changing contribution. My own agenda was to motivate them to practice in the off-season. A typical stanza might be like the one I wrote for Shuree.

*Shuree could sure play the wing*
*And could pass the ball with a zing*
*She could always defend*
*And by season's end*
*She could do most anything.*

Or one of my verses about Tessa, the most aggressive player on my team and truly a team leader, who seemed to bridge girls' hoops and the business world:

*Talent-rich Tessa's not bashful*
*Her tenacious defense is 'brashful'*
*If she harnesses this mania*
*Throughout her academia*
*Her future will be most 'cashful'*

My poetry was bad, but the recognition is what counted.

In his recent book *The Takeaway,* written with his daughter Karyn, Orlando Magic executive Pat Williams presents life lessons for his daughter. One lesson was "There are no giants." The message: perception of other "giants" can intimidate young girls and diminish their confidence in succeeding. There is no better example of that than my fourth-grade NJB All Star team of 2008, who won the Silicon Valley Regional and made it to the Nationals. We won our first game against a very good St. Joseph, Missouri team, and on Saturday night faced a team from Los Angeles. During warm-ups I noticed that if my girls were not either making the lay-up, passing to the shooter or getting the rebound, they were gazing at the other end. At that end was the tallest fourth-grade girl in the history of humankind. She was every bit of five feet ten inches; our tallest girl was my five-foot-two Dagney. I went out to the court and tried to keep the girls' eyes off the "giant." True confession: I had a hard time, myself, keeping my eyes off the giant, and was alarmed that she was not only tall but also (unlike other girls who grow early) very coordinated, with good hand skills. Frankly, I was not sure how we could stop her.

But one thing I learned long ago about coaching is that you cannot build your team's confidence to slay the dragon unless you as a coach exude that confidence, at least in their eyes.

So I pulled the girls off the floor from warm-ups early and addressed the issue head on. I told them that while this girl was tall and talented, the rest of the team was average and not as good as our ten girls. I asked Dagney how many rebounds and putbacks the tall girl would get if she boxed her out on every shot. Dagney, already accepting that she would have this frightening defensive assignment, admitted, "None." I asked the girls how many baskets the tall girl would score if we never let her have the ball. I asked Lauren, our star point guard, that if she pressured their point guard on defense and stayed in her face, how many passes she would be able to make to the tall girl. I asked Maegan that if her girl was on the weak side and Delaney was pressuring the ball handler, would there be any need to guard her girl when she could help Dagney keep the tall girl from getting the ball. I asked Jessica, Sydney and Julia, who tended to be fearless, the same question, and I could see in their eyes that they were already plotting to help on defense. I reminded them that one strong player cannot beat ten good girls who play as a team. I reminded them that we just beat the St. Josephs, Missouri team that had better overall players, because we played as a team. I stressed that at the end of the game, the winning team will not be the one with the best players but the one that played best.

I continued the "team beats one giant" theme throughout the game. Though we were intimidated into a horrible shooting night (every girl thought the tall girl would block her shot), we eked out the win 19-17 by playing incredible team defense. We went on to take second in the Nationals—and on that Saturday night, the girls learned a little about not letting fear control them.

They left the court at the NJB Nationals knowing that giants can indeed be beaten, especially when one has the help of teammates, of friends. The life lesson was that perception does not have to be reality; there are ways to conquer giants, be they difficult classes, bullies, illnesses or other setbacks. The lesson for me was that if I believe, and can convince the girls that not only can we win but that I *expect* to win, the confidence is contagious.

The same teamwork ethic and human nature exists in business. If the manager of a challenging project can not only provide guidance to complete on schedule and on budget but also display the utmost confidence in his/her team to do so, there is a much better chance of succeeding. And even giant companies can be beaten by small companies working together as a team against the giant's weaknesses. Witness Tesla taking an exciting, overbooked electric sports car to market at the same time General Motors declared bankruptcy. This was a small team working together to exploit the weaknesses of the automotive giants.

Another lesson I learned from coaching girls basketball was the value of the unexpected "thank you". I once coached a fourth grader, Emily who was talented but extremely reserved. She barely uttered a phrase to me the entire season. But at the end of season party she silently handed me a thank you card that included a note more poetic than any poem I had ever written for my girls. I still have the card. A couple years later I lost DB, a very talented athlete on my All Net team, due to soccer conflicts. I was not surprised as she was a soccer superstar. What did surprise me was the email I got from her mother who not only informed me DB would not be trying out for the team but thanked me profusely for the year's experience and the basketball skills her daughter had gained. And I thought she was playing hoops just to stay in shape for soccer. Unexpected thank yous…what a wonderful gift.

So as I've stated, life lessons go both ways, to the girls and to the coaches. One year in a club league, I had a talented girl who was reserved but seemed so happy at practices. She was a good athlete with wonderful potential. I wanted to tell her single mom to check out some development camps, but never seemed to catch her after practice. One Saturday after our game, I saw this young athlete standing alone outside the gym door, under the overhang avoiding the rain. There was another game going on inside and I decided it was best not to leave her alone, so I sent my daughter ahead with Dana and waited with my player. I hadn't talked to her much, other than hoops and basketball vocabulary, so I took advantage of the time to learn more about her. Time passed without her mother or anyone else showing up to pick her up. I learned that she looked forward to basketball more than anything else each week. I learned that she had our team picture above her bed, along with a poster of Jennifer Azzi, Stanford basketball star turned pro. She also told me she kept track of all her points from game to game, which I found amusing, as I did the same thing at her age. I found out that she had never been to a college or professional game but read about them regularly in the *Mercury News.*

After twenty minutes, I asked her who was supposed to pick her up.

"I think my mom."

"Would you like to call her?"

"Well, she's really busy today."

"Well, we are all busy, but she must know she should pick you up?"

"Yeah, except today's she's really busy, she's getting married."

*"Yeah, she might be a little busy today…..."*

While there are guidelines that coaches should not take players home from games and practices without another adult, I felt that a daughter missing her mother's wedding would be grounds for a policy exception. We ran to my car in the rain and she directed me to her mother's apartment. As I sat in my car in the parking lot and through my windshield wipers watched her into her third-floor apartment door, I thought, *"This is Los Gatos, California, where one daughter of a single working mother who loves basketball is not getting 100% of parental support, certainly the rare exception here. With her new dad, hopefully that will change. What about all the inner city kids, domestic and international, who love hoops and get no support? Who is helping them?"*

For the first time since my initial California sports cultural shock transition, I left the California culture and took my frame of reference back to the 60s in southern Indiana, where basketball was *the* most important thing for many kids. We *lived* for it. And I realized that I already had the answer to my earlier question. My life lesson was realizing that coaching my daughters' teams was not really community service; after all, I preferred it over most things that I do. I had to go beyond Los Gatos to the communities that needed more than basketball coaches: they needed teachers who could help with things like vocabulary, role models who could provide kids direction by example, substitute parents who can teach right from wrong before the kids have to make the decision on their own. Providing that role became my personal plan. I am sure my player had no idea that she brought me to that conclusion.

The *San Jose Mercury News* reported how basketball brought life itself to a young girl. While playing her sophomore year on the Santa Teresa High School basketball team, Marisol Gonzalez began suffering stomach pains and saw her weight drop from 135 to 89 pounds. She was suffering from superior mesenteric artery syndrome and it was taking her life. While bed bound in the hospital, Marisol kept thinking about her team and her desire to return to the court. She even ventured from the hospital in a wheelchair to join her teammates at one of the practices. After four months of feeding tubes, she began to gain back her weight. She made it back to her team, and as a senior was voted team captain.

"Basketball was her life and it gave her something to strive for," remarked her coach, Sean Peterson.[2] You can't ask more from a sport than that.

[1] The Last Word, The Week, July 3, 2009, pp 44&45.
[2] *San Jose Mercury News*, June 21, 2009.

# 9

## LOOKING BACKWARD, LOOKING FORWARD

*"My responsibility is geting all my players playing for the name on the front of the jersey, not the one on the back."*

— Unknown

*It's Friday night, February 10, 2021 in Los Gatos, California. A fifth-grade girls' game between St. Simon's and St. Mary's enters the fourth quarter. The score is tied and emotions are rising in the bleachers on both sides of the new Howley Hall. Two St. Mary's mothers are in the back row watching their daughters try to stop Simon's three-on-two fast break.*

*"Beat her to the baseline, Olivia!" yells Olivia's mother, Karen, in a thick British accent. "You've got to move your feet, love!" After Olivia stops the dribbler at the baseline she blocks the opponent's shot out of bounds to keep the score tied. "Superb D!" Olivia's mother shouts again. Karen turns to another mother new to St Mary's that year and says, "Dreadful pity, that foul call on your Avery, she had all ball."*

*The new mother thanks Karen for the concern regarding Avery's foul and asks, "How did you and Alasdair end up here at St. Mary's?"*

*"Well, it was fate. Alasdair and I were renting a small apartment in Los Gatos when we first came to America and one night, walking with our friends, we discovered St. Mary's. We actually found what we considered a most peculiar athletic activity, a game called basketball, going on at this very site. Seeing the girls on the floor, the school spirit, the smiling, engaging faces in the crowd, we were captivated, and not just with the game but over time with what was clearly a community of warm, endearing families – HEY ref!" Her voice is heard across the floor. "Number 16 is setting up camp in the paint! You must call three seconds, c'mon!"*

I may have mentioned before that I love basketball and I love my three daughters. My hope in writing this book is that you enjoy sharing the journey that combination gave me. My hope for you basketball or other youth sport coaches is that you pick up a couple of ideas that will help make your players' and your own experiences more rewarding. I hope you have learned like I did that the objective is not to be a winning coach but to coach a winning *team* and that highly competitive coaches like me can realize that some mellowing out is not only good for the players but, frankly, makes you a better person. I hope that people remember the priority of the kids' development first and winning second, and that winning, physical and mental development, and old-fashioned fun can all coexist. And I hope the anecdotes serve as a good reminder of both the innocence and impressionability of the minds of grade-school girls.

When I started this journey I was yelling at referees and losing sleep over lost games. In the course of the journey I became enthralled with watching Sydney sing in musical productions. Now I find the personal development side of youth sports more interesting than the games themselves. I have to say that despite the near relapse with the cheating coach at the deli, my OCCD has been in remission for the last eight years. The mental anguish of Casey's knee injury at such a ripe young age was the biggest antidote to my ailment.

Recently I was concerned about my All Net girls's lack of aggressiveness in a game at Gilroy that we were winning easily. It was Gilroy's first year as an All Net team and the

Los Gatos girls were hitting most of their shots including "threes". But at the end of the game I noticed our girls stood almost as still as statues as a couple Gilroy girls hit layups. After the game I told the girls how "letting up" in any game can lead to bad habits and we needed to be 100% for our next game against Redwood City. When I looked at Sophie and asked her why she did not try to stop the layup at the end of the game she looked up with her sad eyes and replied, "Because I felt sorry for them and they were so nice." When I found myself suddenly smiling I realized two things, that I was truly getting cured from my OCCD and Sophie and her teammates were wonderful girls. No danger of a Covenant 100-0 game with this group.

Now, as I enter my final years of coaching Dagney, I hope I can be a positive mentor for her and her teammates. These wonderful girls whom I have coached for the last twelve years have helped me recover from my OCCD. I realized that a year ago, when I heard an excellent NJB coach talking about the girls he coached who would go on to star in high school and college. While this is possible for some of my girls, I find myself hoping they have all learned much more than the game of hoops.

Casey called recently from her dorm room to say she'd hit four "threes" in a pickup game of all guys at the university recreational gym; she said they were blown away by her prowess. I told her I only wished I could have seen her game—and that she should try to get a D.C. internship and get into an Obama pickup game. Back here in California, as I enter the final stretch of my coaching journey, my hope for all the girls I coached is not that they make it to the WNBA, Division I, Obama pickup games or even high school basketball teams. The statistics we discussed earlier work against most of those categories. I learned from Casey that the girls who make it to Division I sports are those who love sporting competition over everything else, who welcome physical contact with an opponent, and who watch that round analog classroom clock in anticipation of that day's game and not just recess sports. They are the ones who want to win at all costs, sometimes at the expense of personal injury, as in Casey's experience. I have come to realize that this is a single digit percentage of the girls that a coach like me will mentor.

Unlike my fellow NJB coach, my goals are now much more humble given the education the girls have given me. The most rewarding experience for me is to watch the girls develop into wonderful young women. This is an experience I would trade for nothing. As far as my personal goals, maybe I will eventually complete an entire message and strategy in a sixty-second timeout. Or better, maybe I will complete an entire motivational speech that actually inspires the girls as much as cool warm-up attire. Maybe I can finally find the opportunity to coach those who need mentors more than the kids in Los Gatos.

Maybe when asked about playing for coach Charlie my girls will say it was a lot of fun. Maybe because of my role, Lauren has taken up any grievances with a friend in private. Maybe Becky has never made an insensitive comment about someone's weight or appearance. Maybe, when one of my girls gets cut from her high school team, another ex-teammate who switched on picks for her is there to comfort her. Maybe if one of my girls is nervously waiting for MRI results, her past 5th grade All Net teammate holds the same hand she high-fived after a key lay up. Maybe Stephanie continues on the rest of her life defending those who are picked on and becomes a social worker. Maybe all my girls are using *ubiquitous* and *ambidextrous* in non-basketball sentences. Maybe, because of my coaching and their playing experience, they now get fired up for a Warriors - Lakers game. Maybe they don't miss a single home hoops game in college, men's or women's. Maybe they paint their faces for the big high school or college conference rivalry game. Or maybe they get those special goose bumps on opening day of March Madness, when their school finally makes the BIG DANCE, the greatest spectacle in sports!

And later on, if one of them at a party around a hoops game on TV yells, "C'mon ref, that was a moving pick!" maybe a special guy will take notice and think, *"Hey, that girl is not just hot, but she's got game!"* And maybe that leads to the love of her life. Now that would make all the years I coached worthwhile.

SPORTS

## Wildcats are Winners

The Los Gatos Wildcats, a girls 4th-grade all-stars basketball team, defeated all-star teams from Foothill, Almaden, Palo Alto and Redwood City to win the Silicon Valley NJB Tournament, then won three of four games in Orange County to finish second in the NJB Nationals. Team members

## Wildcats Win Net Title

The Wildcats, a Los Gatos 5th grade girls All Net NJB basketball team, won the Thanksgiving Classic tournament

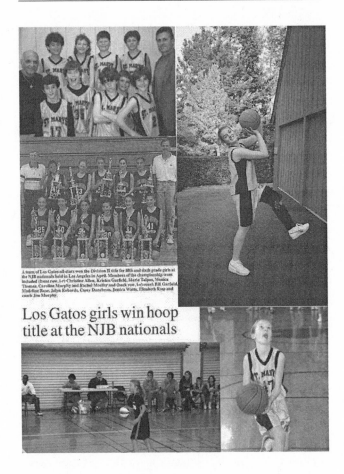

A team of Los Gatos all-stars won the Division II title for fifth and sixth grade girls at the NJB nationals held in Los Angeles in April. Members of the championship team included (front row, l-r) Christine Allen, Kristen Garfield, Maria Talpas, Monica Thomas, Caroline Murphy and Rachel Mueller and (back row, l-r) coach Bill Garfield, Madeline Rose, John Robards, Casey Danielsen, Jessica Watts, Elizabeth Rose and coach Jim Murphy.

## Los Gatos girls win hoop title at the NJB nationals

# A

## APPENDIX

# SAMPLE GAME PLAN

**St. Mary's 8th Grade Game Plan** | **Holy Family**

| Pos. | Q1 7:00 | 3:30 | 1:00 | Q2 7:00 | 6:00 | 3:30 | 1:00 | Q3 7:00 | 3:30 | 1:00 | Q4 7:00 | 6:00 | 3:30 | 2:00 (close) | 2:00 (decided) | 1:00 (decided) |
|---|---|---|---|---|---|---|---|---|---|---|---|---|---|---|---|---|
| 5 | Christina | Christina | Janelle | Janelle | Janelle | Beldi/Ch | Christina | Christina | Caroline | Christina | Beldi | Kelsey | Christina | | Caroline | Amanda |
| 4 | Kelsey | Andrea | Amanda | Amanda | Beldi | Sheena | Kelsey | Kelsey | Amanda | Amanda | Janelle | Andrea | Kelsey | | Sheena | Sheena |
| 3 | Caroline | Beaupre | Sheena | Sheena | Amanda | Caroline | Beaupre | Beaupre | Andrea | Kelly | Beaupre | Beaupre | Sheena | | Andrea | Andrea |
| 2 | Genna | Lauren | Genna | Genna | Kelly | Kelly | Casey | Lauren | Kelly | Genna | Genna | Lauren | Genna | Genna | Genna | Kelly |
| 1 | Casey | Casey | Beldi | Beldi | Genna | Casey | Andrea | Casey | Genna | Kelly | Lauren | Casey | Casey* | Casey** | Andrea | Kelly |
| Def. | mtm fc | mtm fc | 2 1 z | 2 1 z | mtm tc | mtm tc | mtm fc | mtm fc | mtm fc | mtm fc | mtm fc | mtm fc | mtm fc | mtm fc | 2 1 z | 2 1 z |

Notes within grid: "Genna if", "we are", "leading by 4", "*", "**", "Kelly for / if game", "casey at / decided", "5 min if / Lauren", "game won"

Substitution / defensive notes:
- full court / middle
- Sheena in full court.
- middle on 212
- throw in/inc. Sheena
- full court | middle

| | |
|---|---|
| def. | 1. Guards pressure ball for steal, forwards front their girls. |
| def. | 2. Forwards switch if our guard is beaten; beaten guard switches to forward's girl. |
| off. | 3. Guards move ball up quickly before zone sets up, penetrate paint, layup or dish. |
| off. | 4. Casey penetrate paint for double team, open player at Casey for ball. |
| press | 5. DO NOT GUARD INBOUND PASSER, keep ball out of middle. |
| press | 6. 2-12 press starts at the throw in and simply shifts up the court |

## SAMPLE REPORT CARD

| Basketball Skills Assessment | | | | |
|---|---|---|---|---|
| **5th Grade Girls All Net** | | | | XXXXX |
| | **1** | **2** | **3** | **Comments** |
| Passing | | x | | Needs to put more ZIP! on the passes, sometimes does not pass away from the defense |
| Receiving Pass | | x | | Needs to pop in and out to get open. |
| Individual Defense | | x | | Can get many more steals and layups |
| Team Defense | | | x | Great job of leaving girl to stop or block shot of another player |
| Rebounding | | x | | Good now because of height.  Needs to jump higher and box out. |
| Shooting | | x | | Excellent bank shots in close, just need to practice free throws and longer shots |
| Creating the shot | x | | | Needs to SELL the head fake and then drive, SELL the foot fake and then drive |
| Layups | | | x | Don't slow up to make the layup.  Finally using the left hand. |
| Dribbling | | x | | Need to protect the dribble by looking over the shoulder |
| Team Offense | | x | | Does a great job of seeing open girls, sometimes does not see the defender when passing |
| Court Sense | | | x | Knows the game as well as any 5th grader |
| Conditioning | | | x | Soccer has her in good shape |
| Speed | | | x | Probably the fastest in the entire league.  USE IT! |
| | | | | 1 - Needs Improvement |
| | | | | 2 - All Net 5th Grade Level |
| | | | | 3 - Top All Net 5th Grade Level |

# SAMPLE TEAM POEM

## The Lynx of 2007-2008

Danielle has hoops in her genes
It shows in how she sets screens
Beyond her skill with the banker
We all had a hanker
For how she could jump with extreme

Nicole learned defense from soccer
She clearly is a ball hawker
But in her last game
She did it all with fame
As a scorer, stealer, and shot blocker

Emily's loves to compete
On the wing her speed can't be beat
Anticipating the pass
She turns on the gas
Steals, and gets the layup to complete

Depending on Cailin's a good bet
And we owe her a special debt
We were pleased so much
Against LG2 in the clutch
Her free throw was nothin but net

A fine shooting guard was Delaney
Her hustling defense was zaney
We got the most for her pounds
Even offensive rebounds
But mostly we'll remember the THREE

Now Caroline had much more
Than the desire to play D and score
After getting the rebound
And passing to the outbound
She was the first one down the floor

Dagney will beat the defender
Even those from the other gender
Her assists were great
But what our opponents still hate
Are the shots that were "returned to sender"

There's so much that Dani can do
Always a threat for the two
On defense, "Miss Dismember"
And we all will remember
How she stopped Gilroy's #2

Maegan came to dominate the low post
And she is never one to boast
Her play in the paint
Made defenders faint
And made Gilroy and LG2 toast.

## ABOUT THE AUTHOR

Charlie Duncheon, known as "Hoosier Daddy" among his California friends, grew up in the hills of southern Indiana, where basketball was king. His love for the game, both as a player and later as a coach, inspired his first book. An engineer and successful executive in high technology companies, he expects initial readers of *Reflections* to surpass the combined readership of his technical papers and articles on robotics, which, in his words, "won't take much." Charlie resides in Los Gatos, California with his wife Dana, daughters Casey, Sydney and Dagney, cats Denzel and Grey Cat, Guinea Pig Cosmo Kramer, and Bichon Frise dog Louie the Loser.

## EXCERPTS FROM REVIEWS

**Archbishop Mitty High School Girls Basketball Coach Sue Phillips:**" ... enjoyable read that provides both an insightful and humerous perspective into coaching youth sports.

**Yelp Critic Don O'Neill**: " ...a real gem...I laughed out loud or had a continuous smile while reading *Reflections*."

**Oklahoma CPA and Youth Coach Andrew Schmidt:** "I was truly moved to tears a few times and more so to laughs of great shared experiences...I've since bought 10 books for coaches and friends."

**Parents of Division I Athletes, John and Neen Holm:**"Anyone who knows Charlie will not be surprised to see that he has added "brilliant author" to his long list of successful endeavors. Thanks for the fun read. Looking forward to the movie!"

**Others:** "What a great book!" "Great story telling!" " ... what is important in life." "Made me both laugh and cry." "It blew me away!...I loved it!" "The challenges of coaching and being a parent were beautifully written. How he intertwined his life, the life of his girls, and the journey of personal growth was a joy to read." " ...a must read!" "You will pass it on and they will pass it on..."

**Reviews at charlieduncheon.posterous.com**

Published by FastPencil

http://www.fastpencil.com